THE MACTOR'S GUIDE

A How To Guide For

Model/Actors

Benz Veal

Legacy Footprints
An Imprint of Legacy Footprints Publishing

ACKNOWLEDGMENTS

Behind every successful person, there was a team of people that played a part in their success. I would like to take the time and give thanks to the individuals that played a part in my success, no matter how big or small.

First, I would like to thank my Mother and Father because without them, I wouldn't be here. I especially would like to thank my father for planting the seed of modeling and acting in my mind when I was seventeen. I would like to thank Deatrice Lockhart, Rich M, Anneliese Salien, Bryan Edwards, Jamil Whitlow, Jeanette Whitlow, X Factor Modeling Troupe, Charles Talley, Vanecia Carr, Tony Lockett, Jamayne Harris, Kyphi Cordero, Bunim Murray Productions, Natalie Nunn, Stevie Boi, Andra Juarez, Rosalind Rice, Toni Steed, Ben Oduro, Simona Sheinkman, Jolie Bergeron, NYMMG, Marc Rutherford, Shawna McCormack, Thomas Winslow, Ray Volant, Bella Agency, Wilmarie Sena, Jessica Ngan, Frine Medrano, Jenny Vongsa, Elizabeth Anderson, Amora Grinan, Deiondra Sanders, Kalilah Harris, Brittney Flemons, Ben Roberts, Greg Avila, Jodi Benjamin, Mbali Adisa, Kamey Butler. Nasco Mihaylov, Grace Models, Jason, Tim Ayers, Anna Trilleras, Model Club, Chrystian Dennis, Ashley Bellamy, Maleeka Clary, Asianna Sanders, Sanaa Jaman, Ceasar V, Elaine Tsang, Daffany Clark, Kim Smoot, Cathie Yamaguchi, Marcus Yamaguchi, Ashanna Bri, Royce V, Benjamin Selle, Lillian Cierra Mayer, Jennifer Smoot, Pamela Ricardo, Boston Casting, CP Casting, Matthew Hagerty, Katelyn Kennedy, Anne Kohlmeier, Katelyn Landry, my family, friends and everyone that I may have forgotten to mention. You all played a significant part in the advancement of my career and I am truly grateful.

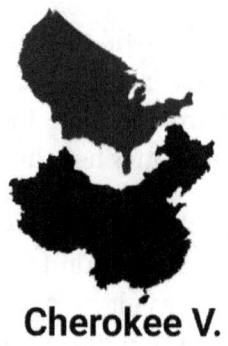

Cherokee V.

ISBN: 978-1-7337008-0-1

Copyright © 2018 Benz Veal all rights reserved. No part of this publication may be reproduced, distributed or transmitted in any form or by any means, including photocopying, recording or other electronic or mechanical methods, without the prior written permission of the publisher, except in the case of brief quotations embodied in reviews and certain other non-commercial uses permitted by copyright law.

CONTENTS

Preface

1

Before the Agent

5

Chapter 1

How to Sign With an Agency

9

Chapter 2

How to Win in Auditions

21

Chapter 3

How to Survive Modeling and Acting Full Time

57

PREFACE

I am a full-time model and actor in the entertainment industry. I started my professional career in April of 2011 when I appeared on my first ever TV show. When the show aired, I quit my job at Abercrombie & Fitch and decided that I was going to model and act full time. Before modeling and acting, I was a business major in college with an entrepreneurial spirit. I worked as a bartender, retail sales associate, etc. I always worked multiple jobs and secured various streams of income. I was what you would've considered, the ultimate hustler. Focusing all of my energy into one career path, with only one source of income was a difficult challenge but one I was willing to accept.

Why did I write this book?

People have been suggesting that I write a book for many years, but I couldn't figure out what type. I didn't know if I wanted to write about my life in the industry or about my life in general. One reason is that I'm aging and want to start writing down my experiences before I forget them. I also would find myself sharing advice with other models and actors on set that wanted to know my secrets. I'm always coaching other talent and helping them obtain work in their careers. Lastly, I became exhausted answering questions about how to get started in the business, sign with an agent, etc. So I decided that I was going to write a "**How To Guide**."

What's my objective?

To give the aspiring model/actor a guide to help jump-start their career and give seasoned individuals some tips that they can use as well. I didn't have a lot of people in the industry to provide me with advice along the way. No one reached out to take me under their wing and show me the way. I didn't get a cheat sheet for the test. There aren't many people in this world that want to help you achieve greatness. Instead of repeating the trend of not supporting new talent in fear that they will take your place, I've decided to be the cheat sheet. I want the up and coming models and actors to surpass me. I wanted this guide to be a short read and straight to the point. As soon as the readers finish reading the book, they can start implementing what they've learned.

What is a MACTOR?

A Mactor is an individual who was a model first and then transitioned into acting. They are able to work in both professions. I first heard the term when an actor friend of mine commented on my Facebook page. I liked it and decided to use it in the title of my book.

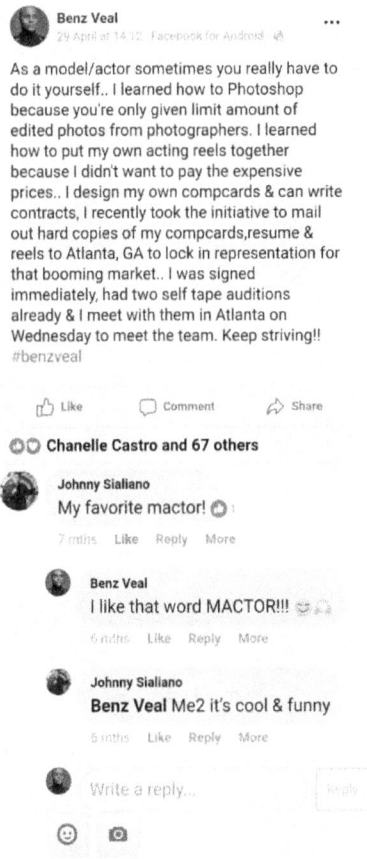

BEFORE THE AGENT

People always asked how did I get into modeling and acting or how did I sign with a Modeling/Talent agency. Well, there are a few actions one must take before searching for an agency.

THE REASON

Before thinking about signing to an agency or asking someone who is already an established Mactor this process, you must ask yourself some questions. **WHY** do **YOU** want to be a Mactor? Is it something that you always wanted to be? Is it the fame that attracts you? Is it the money? What exactly is your reason? I know for me, it was about proving a point. I used to look at models in magazines, on billboards and thought to myself *"I can do that"*; however, the main trigger that gave me the insatiable desire to pursue this career was an incident that happened in 2006. A friend of mine and high school classmate suggested that I take some modeling type of photos. I thought to myself, *"why not? I'm not doing anything else of great importance"*.

We did the photo shoot, and I uploaded the photos to Model Mayhem like any other aspiring model. While my photos were on the website, I was contacted by an agent in New York. He said that King Magazine had a shoot coming up and he would like to submit me for it. If I book the job, I would have to come to New York. Of course, I didn't have a problem with going to New York if that meant that I could become a professional model by booking my first job right away. I booked the job for King Magazine's "head to toe" section. In this section, you don't see the models face, arms or hands. Everything is invisible, but they use the frame of your body.

After the shoot, I went back to Charlotte, North Carolina and the Agent never sent my portion of the money, which was $125 dollars. That angered me to the point that I thought to myself, ***"Since he didn't pay me, I'm going take this Modeling stuff serious and really get in shape. He is going to see me on billboards and magazines across the nation."*** So my reason was to prove a point but what is yours?

THE HOW'S

After you figure out the reason you want to become a Mactor, the next step is to ask yourself some Hows. How serious are you and how much are you willing to sacrifice for this career? This is going to determine how much effort you're eager to contribute to being successful in this industry. You previously read that I was serious enough to stop what I was doing and get on a bus to New York to go shoot a campaign. The round trip bus ride was around $88 at that time, and the job paid $125.

Is the profit worth it to you? Are you serious enough to move to a random city for this life? Are you willing to sacrifice going out to party versus spending hours in the gym or studying your craft? Are you ready to sacrifice eating all the joyous unhealthy foods and maintain a healthy diet, so that you can look your best at all times? Are you willing to sacrifice your dating life so that your career can have your undivided attention? Are you ready to sacrifice your reliable income to pursue this career? Are you willing to sacrifice your stability of a home and possibly be homeless? It's a strong possibility that it can happen.

I ask you these questions because I've made these choices and still implement them today. What are the results? I've appeared on numerous billboards, published in several magazines, co-starred in movies and TV shows.

ARE YOU READY?

Are you ready to be repeatedly told **NO!**? In this line of work, you'll be told no more than yes. Some people weren't told yes until after many years of pursuing this career. Are you ready to be told you're too fat or too skinny? For years I've kept my body in top shape, yet, one suit line said that I was too small and my agent said that I needed to eat a hamburger.

Are you ready to be told that you're too short or too tall? You have to have thick skin to survive in this industry. Are you prepared to be told that you aren't good enough? Will that motivate or break you? Are you ready for everyone to think that you've made it big time as soon as they see you on any publications, even though you may be financially struggling? Many people don't understand how the industry works.

Are you ready for some of the people that you know from your hometown say that you've changed because you're on TV and billboards now? Are you prepared for the pressure of when you do make it in the industry and have to maintain your celebrity status because everyone has expectations of you? Are you ready for the low times in your career when people whom you thought were your friends, disappear because you can no longer benefit them? Are you ready to be called a bum? To get a "**REAL**" job, be homeless, couch surf, sleep in your car? Are you **REALLY READY?**

If so, then **CONGRATULATIONS!!!** We welcome you to our circle. I hope that this guide will help you along your journey in this challenging yet rewarding industry. Prepare to have the time of your life! This journey is filled with an emotional rollercoaster like never before. There will be ups, downs, cries, laughter, stress, and peace. Embrace all of it because it will make a great story to tell. Now, let's begin.

Chapter 1

HOW TO SIGN WITH AN AGENCY

In this section of the book, we will discuss what an agency/agent is, why you need one, how they can benefit you and some tactics that you can use to boost your chances in getting signed to one.

WHAT IS A TALENT AGENCY?

A talent agency is a company that specializes in finding their models and actors potential work. They also serve as a medium for companies who are looking for models or actors for their projects. An agent is an individual who usually works for an agency. They are your voice, hype man, secretary, and power of attorney for companies who are seeking to employ you. They are your bounty hunters for those companies that try not to pay you and translators if you are not versed in reading contracts.

They are your guardian to protect you from companies who want to use your likeness for malicious use or any use without your prior consent and proper compensation. However, these agents aren't for free. You will pay a fee for their service. Most agencies charge a fee of 10% to 20% for every job that you book with them.

WHY DO YOU NEED ONE OR SEVERAL?

Are four arms better than two? Imagine how many tasks you can accomplish with four arms versus two. While you're busy working on yourself, agents are marketing to hundreds of potential clients for you. Most of you don't have personal relationships with casting directors or producers to get directly booked for a job, but an agency does. Imagine if you have a total of 8 agencies worldwide marketing you in their cities to find potential work. Meanwhile, you're sleeping; out on dates, working a modeling/acting job or your day job. Need I say more?

HOW CAN THEY BENEFIT YOU?

Simple, they'll negotiate for higher pay if they think that a company is trying to pay you less than what you're worth. There is nothing more gratifying than receiving a phone call from your agent telling you that he/she negotiated more money for you. They can open doors that you'll never be able to on your own until you're a supermodel or an A-list actor. Now that you know what an agency/agent is let's move on to the main course.

DO YOUR HOMEWORK

You have to do your homework and figure out what do you want to be in this industry. Do homework on your body and find out certain things about yourself and where you might fit in. Figure out if you want to be a high fashion model or a commercial lifestyle model, if you're a leading man actor with a face that everyone loves, a character actor with a look some people would like with a likable personality or a face only a mother could love as a villain.

Study certain people that you admire in the industry that you may want to model your career after. When I first started out, I wanted to be a high fashion model. I started researching and calling agencies asking their height and weight requirements for male models.

They told me between 5'11 and 6'2. I told the assistant that I was 6'1 and 170 lbs and she said that was the perfect height. I checked that off the list and started researching high fashion models. I noticed that they all had prominent cheekbones and sharp jawlines. Some were built solid, but many were slim. I knew that I couldn't become that slim because of my body frame. I researched Tyson Beckford because he is more of my body type and size. I studied him and started mimicking his poses from his photo shoots.

I wanted to duplicate similar success. After studying a lot of model's physiques and facial bone structures, I began my training in the gym to become what they were.

YOUR APPEARANCE WILL GET YOU THE PLAY AND YOUR MIND WILL GET YOU PAID

This is an old saying that my dad instilled in all his children since we were young. This is something you have to fully understand, believe and apply in your life every day. In the previous title, I mentioned how I started molding myself to look like the other high fashion models that I wanted to be like. Well, the title of this topic is the reason.

Once people started seeing me as a model or suggested that I should get into modeling, I knew that I was on the right track. It only makes sense to look like what you want to be. You can't be a leading man actor without first looking like one, and the same goes for everything else. Once a modeling agency identifies you as a model, the easier it will be for them to sign you. We want simple and straightforward, not complicated and challenging.

The very first agent that I ever had said; *"you should look like a model at all times because you never know who may be watching."* That statement is authentic. Sometimes opportunities will fall right into your lap by looking your best all the time. Would you rather pull a diamond out of the rough and do all the cleaning and polishing before wearing or selling it or would you like a polished diamond that is retail ready?

It's exciting for agencies to meet a potential signee that arrives in top shape and has a portfolio of photos to showcase their modeling skills. It means that they don't have to do much work versus molding you from scratch. Your chances of getting signed are high, and they might start submitting you for projects immediately. When you talk to agents, maintain a happy medium of being confident yet humble. No one likes a complete A** hole, and no one likes an overly timid individual. Be sure of what you want to do with your career and where you want to go.

The sky is the limit, and if you can convince them to imagine the atmosphere with you, then you're on your way, my friend. A little humor can take you a long way, so be funny. A lot of times, agents can be coldhearted when meeting them, but that doesn't mean you have to be. Put on that smile and charm. Your appearance will get you the play (the agency is interested in meeting you and thinking about signing you because of how you look and carry yourself) and your mind will get you paid (having confidence in where you want to go in your career and having a great personality with some charm in your conversation).

MAKE YOUR PHOTOS COUNT

When it comes to taking photos, I'm particular. I'm not a fan of taking pointless images. I told the second photographer that I ever worked with that I only want to shoot concepts that look like magazine advertisements.

It only made sense to shoot this way because A) my goal was to be in magazines and on billboards. B) If I could convince agencies that when they look at my photos, they're looking at an image that could be a magazine ad or on a billboard, then they would see my potential and sign me. We created visual concepts that resembled ad campaigns. I added various company logos on some pictures, and people thought that they were real ad campaigns. Be unconventional and *shoot campaign ad style!*

Study ad campaigns, mimic their styles and add them to your portfolio. When agencies see this, they can tell that you took the initiative to understand what their clients want. When an aspiring model asks me for help with their photo shoots, I send them ad campaigns as a reference to photograph in that type of concept. There is nothing like showing clients that you already understand what they want and agents know this as well.

Only do photo shoots that are going to strengthen your portfolio. Don't shoot with every photographer in the world because it's free. You may become overexposed and unwanted. A free photo shoot doesn't always mean it's the best. Remember, you get what you pay for. If they're willing to shoot some of your concepts in exchange for some of theirs, then fine. Show up to the agency with what I have told you, and it will increase your chances of being signed.

ALWAYS BE WILLING TO RELOCATE

If you travel to New York, Los Angeles or any other market seeking representation, they are going to ask you one to two questions. 1. Do you live in whatever city you are meeting them in? If you say no, they may ask; 2. Are you willing to relocate? If you are serious about your career, you will say **YES** you live in whatever city you're taking the meeting in and work on the living arrangements later. If you become afraid or nervous and say no, definitely say you're willing to relocate.

Agencies do not like signing a model or actor who they can't submit to auditions immediately and trust that they will be there at a moment's notice.

HAVE A MONOLOGUE READY

When you go into a meeting for a talent agency, there's a chance that they will ask you to perform a monologue. Pick a monologue that you're comfortable with and can present with your own personality. Avoid mimicking the character in the movie, play or TV show that you saw it on. They are looking for originality, not a copycat.

BE READY TO COLD READ
A COMMERCIAL SCRIPT

I have personally gone into an agency, and they've asked me to go into another room and look at a script for a few minutes. After a few minutes, they asked me to read it in front of a camera with my own style. They want to see your personality and can you deliver the punch lines in the ad naturally. Be yourself and practice commercial scripts in your spare time. I signed with that agency after the cold read because I was prepped. You know what to expect now, so get to it!

Cold Reading: *1.The reading aloud of a script or performative text, as for television, theater, or film, with little or no rehearsal, practice, or study in advance. (the free dictionary)*

YOUR WORK SPEAKS FOR ITSELF

Once you've obtained some work, it's easier to sign with another agency. Why? Because you've proven that you're a marketable talent. In 2011 I walked in New York Fashion Week for Stevie Boi eyewear collection. After the runway show was over, I was approached by two agents representing NYMMG. They expressed their interest in signing me to their agency.

I was thrilled because that was the main reason I went to New York. I had just moved to LA and was trying to put together a plan. The reality TV show that I was on finished airing and I decided that I wanted to pursue acting and modeling again.

I really liked the cameras, lights and the great feeling it gave me, so I wanted to nurture that feeling. While living in LA, one of the cast mates from the reality TV show connected me with Stevie Boi. He said that I could walk in his show. I paid my own airfare and went to NYC. I went to experience New York Fashion Week and potentially be discovered by an agency. After the runway show, I went to NYMMG and signed my first ever modeling contract.

One of the agents later revealed to me that he had recognized me from the reality TV show that I was on and was the reason they had an interest in me. He also expressed that he thought I was going to be arrogant because of his prior experience with Reality TV stars. After talking to me and realizing that I was humble and excited to sign with them, they didn't mind that I was returning to LA because they had an office there too.

In 2015, I walked into Model Club in Boston, MA with my portfolio full of many magazine tear sheets from various campaigns of my work. They signed me on the spot. Make sure you always collect your work because **work begets work!!**

EMBRACE YOUR RACIAL AMBIGUITY

Has anyone ever ask you what your ethnicity is? Or they will say: "you look mix, what are you mixed with? You don't look full black or entirely white, what are you mixed with? I've been asked this on several occasions. Embrace your racial ambiguity. Being racially ambiguous is a huge trend. It's a great time to embrace it.

In 2013, I met a young lady at a casting. After the audition was over, we talked, and I explained to her that I wanted to model and act in another country. She told me about Cape Town, South Africa and I said to her that I wanted to go there. She put me in contact with an agent over there, and after a few emails, they signed me. The agency paid for my flight, and I arrived in January 2014. I asked the agent for the reason why they had signed me to the Grace Modeling Agency:

ME: *"When Jodi Benjamin told you about me & you saw my Modeling Portfolio online, why was I signed to Grace Modeling Agency for the South African market?"*

AGENT (Mbali Adisa): *"S.A (South Africa) Market is commercial, and the international client that do shoot here* *often look for racially ambiguous people that are obviously black but could be from any part of the world."*

By looking racially ambiguous, it led to me signing with Grace Models in Cape Town, South Africa and I earned the title of being called an International male model.

HAVE AN AWESOME ONLINE PROFILE

There's a website called LA Casting where many auditions are posted. Independent Mactors can self submit to auditions on there. In September 2011, I returned from New York Fashion Week and signed up for LA casting. In October, I was requested to meet with Bella Agency.

I came into the meeting confident because I recently signed with NYMMG and my portfolio was up to par. I explained to him that the Reality TV show I co-starred on just finished airing and I just returned from New York Fashion Week. I also relayed to him that I had worked hard to get this far in my career and established a fan base.

He signed me on the spot after our meeting was finished. I asked him why did he sign me, and he replied that he's been in the industry for a long time as an agent and model. He said that when he saw my online profile, he knew I had a lot of potential, a universal look and will be in the industry for a long time. Having my best photos online for a casting website, led to me being signed to a modeling agency. Make sure you're advertising your best pictures and resume online. Invest money into the casting websites because you never know who may reach out to you.

THE MACTOR'S GUIDE

Chapter 2

HOW TO WIN IN AUDITIONS

Auditioning is the process in which a Mactor performs in front of the casting director, producer or director for a potential job. This is one of the most stressful parts of your career. If you think trying to sign with an agent was difficult, wait until you're sent on an audition and the pressure starts crawling on your back. If your first audition is through an agency, you might be thinking; "What if I don't book this job, will they release me from their roster? What are they going to ask me in this room? Can I do this? What if I do a terrible job?" etc.

As Mactors, we apply a lot of pressure to ourselves. The auditioning process can be very stressful, especially if you're depending on booking this job to pay your rent. However, **RELAX!!** This is your chance to showcase to the world what you're really made of.

This is your chance to tell that funny story that you always wanted to tell but didn't ever get a chance. Show off those dance moves that you've been practicing in the mirror from watching music videos and showcase your shower singing skills. This is the time to be as goofy as you want to be or portray any character that you always wanted to be. This is one of the few times where someone wants to watch you, hear what you have to say and give you their undivided attention. If they like you for their project, they will hire you.

So what are you stressing about?? Go out there and enjoy yourself!!

I know some will read that last sentence and say "Whatever Benz, easier said than done" I understand. In this chapter, I am going to give you some tools to prepare you so you'll go into these auditions and be the champion that I know all of you are.

It's like going into an exam one morning, but someone gave you the cheat sheet the day before. You walk into the classroom with the most confidence ever and may even have a cocky grin on your face. A lot of us have been there, so I am pretty sure you know what I am talking about. For those who haven't experienced that or understand what I am talking about, imagine that you're a mind reader and you knew the answer to someone's question before they asked and then they ask.

In this section, I will reveal some tips that you can use to increase your chances of booking print advertisements, film and TV roles, and commercials. It has served me well in my career, and I hope that it will do the same for you.

EMBRACE YOUR PERSONALITY

IT CAN TAKE YOU PLACES

The second professional job that I ever booked was the Reality TV show titled *Bad Girls Club "Love Games" Bad Girls Need Love Too season 2*. Many Reality TV shows were cast based on personality types at that time. Love Games was a dating show that incorporated physical and mental competitions. It consisted of 3 Bad Girls and 15 men with different personalities. I remember sitting at home frustrated, trying to figure out what I was going to do with my life. My dad would always say to me *"there's always work at the post office."* I could feel him about to slide a newspaper under the door at any moment, suggesting that it was time to look for a job.

One day I came across a casting on craigslist about dating. The post wanted to know if I was single, looking for love and wouldn't mind traveling to California. It also stated that there would be financial compensation. I decided that I was going to submit to this casting because; I get a chance to go to Hollywood, meet hot women and get paid at the same time. I submitted myself, answered their questions, and I received an email from them to come in for an audition on Saturday, July 17, 2010.

Love Games BOSTON casting - Saturday, July 17th @ 11:00 AM

Inbox

Love Games
to me
7/9/2010 View details

Congratulations!!!

You have been selected to meet with one of our casting directors for: LOVE GAMES

A show from the creators of MTV's The Real World and Oxygen's The Bad Girls Club!

VERY IMPORTANT: Please be sure you bring a copy of this letter with you.

THE MACTOR'S GUIDE

I didn't know what to expect when I entered the room. A young woman was sitting at one end of a long conference table, and the other guys were sitting around the rest of the table. I sat directly across from her. She asked a series of questions and how we would handle the situations. I stayed true to myself and answered all of the questions honestly.

After my responses, she stated that I was a "smooth" one. I was only embracing who I was. I had nothing to lose and everything to gain out of this situation. When it came to dating, they were either going to accept me for who I was or not.

After weeks of filling out paperwork and talking to my references, I was flown out to Hollywood for an interview with the producers. I was finally selected as one of the contestants for the show. After taking a psychological test and reviewing my interviews, they named me "The Smooth Operator." Embrace your personality because you never know where it may take you. I obtained a free trip to Hollywood, CA, met attractive women and co-starred on a Reality TV show.

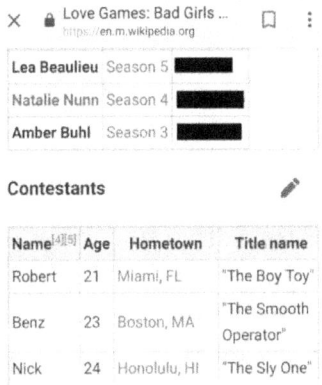

REAL LIFE EXPERIENCES WORK DON'T BE AFRAID TO USE THEM

My first audition as a signed Mactor was a print advertisement for Bud Light Beer. It was for their upcoming NFL Draft. I was nervous but excited. I was nervous because it was my first audition and excited because I wanted to prove myself.

When I walked into the building, I didn't know what to expect. I surveyed the area and read the signs for which audition I was there for. Luckily for me, there wasn't a whole bunch of people in the waiting area. I remember what I wore that day. I had on an army green button up shirt, slim fit blue jeans and brown boots.

The casting director called my name, and I walked into the room. I stood on the line as directed and was asked to state my name and agency. After doing that with a smile, He started explaining what the scenario was and what he wanted me to do. The nervousness began to creep in until I heard him say; *"Imagine your favorite football team is making their last drive down to the touchdown to win the game, and you celebrate the win. I want to see the progression."*

Once he said that all of the nervousness ceased. I imagined Tom Brady from the New England Patriots making that 4th quarter drive to win the game, and I celebrated with all the victory dances. The casting director really enjoyed my performance, and I thanked him for the opportunity. I was happy that I did an excellent job at the audition and represented my agency well.

Some time went by, and I traveled to Detroit, MI, and Monterrey, Mexico. While in Mexico, I received the news that I had booked the Bud Light Campaign. I booked an early flight back to Los Angeles, CA and when I entered the house, I jumped up so high that I almost hit my head on the ceiling and let out a loud yeah. I had officially become a professional working model. Remembering past events that took place in your life and using them to your advantage in an audition, can definitely work in your favor. It enabled me to book my first audition ever in my career.

NEVER RESTATE THE QUESTION IN THE BEGINNING OF YOUR ANSWER

Has someone ever asked; "*What's your favorite food?*" and you reply with; "*My favorite food is...?*" when this happens, it indicates that you're thinking of an answer and casting dislikes this. Casting purposely asks these types of questions to see if you're a quick thinker and if you've been trained. So when a casting director asks "*What is your favorite food?*" your reply should be "*pizza*, continue talking about why it's your favorite food and **END** the conversation with "***that is why pizza is my favorite food.***"

Fortunately for me, I didn't run into this problem for my first few auditions and job bookings before Coach Mike Pointer from ***Hey I saw your commercial*** class, revealed this nugget of information.

HOW TO STAND IN AN AUDITION

Many people don't know how to stand in an audition. They don't know what to do with their hands. Some Mactors will put both of their hands over their crotch like a fig leaf, hold one arm like they've been wounded, keep their arms behind their backs like they were in the military or have their hands on their hip like a superhero. Either one of these stances isn't the best. Make a fist with one hand, cover it with the other hand and hold it over your abdomen or slightly below it. You can break the bond with the two hands while you're speaking but return back to the position when you are done. Practice this in the mirror over and over until it is second nature to you.

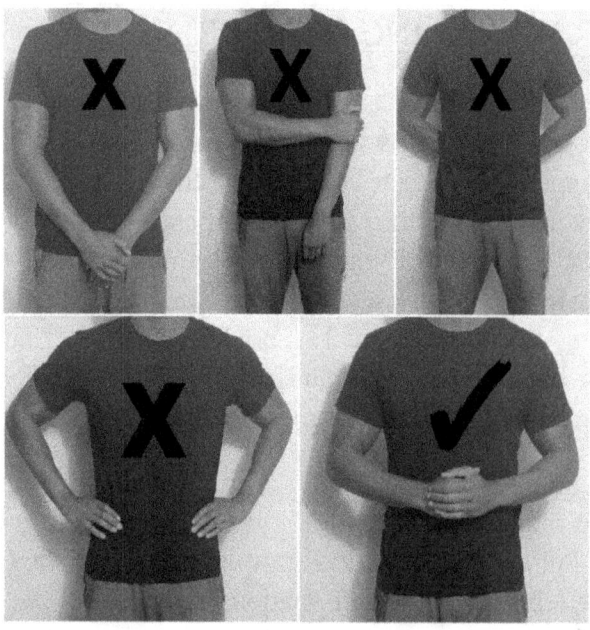

SMILE BEFORE YOU ENTER AND BEFORE YOU LEAVE

In my opinion, the audition starts right before you enter the building where the casting is taking place. You should have a smile on your face right before you go into the building. Greet everyone with a friendly smile. Sometimes there will be a casting associate signing people in, keep that smile flowing. Maintain your smile when you enter the audition room and when you have finished. Whether you think you did a great job or a terrible job, ***KEEP THAT SMILE GOING!!*** The audition isn't over until you're out of the building and in your car, train, taxi or bus. Smiles are contagious, boost other people's day and make you a likable talent among casting.

DON'T REACH YOUR HAND OUT FIRST TO SHAKE ANYONE'S HAND

It is improper to reach your hand out to a casting director, producer, etc. in an audition first for a handshake. You don't know what kind of day they've had. In some casting rooms I've been in, they weren't the most welcoming. They've been sitting through hours of watching good and bad auditions. The last thing you want to do is ruin your audition before it starts. If they're feeling warm and welcoming, they will reach their hand out and make that connection with you first.

MASTERING THE 5 MINUTE POSES

Sometimes when you go into a print audition, they will take 5 quick pictures of you, and you're done. It takes less than 5 minutes. Many Mactors are caught off guard with this. When you walk in, they will ask you to stand on the mark. They will give you an id sheet, ask you to hold it up and take a picture of you holding it. Most of the time they want you to smile holding it.

*This is the **key** to the **natural chuckle smile**; Think of something funny from a past event, how weird the camera person might look today, an odd outfit someone has on, etc. Find the humor in anything that will cause light laughter with at least two ha ha's with teeth showing for the picture. I call this the chuckle smile because it's not quite a full laugh; it's more of a small laugh to yourself.*

After that first picture with the ID sign, they will take another photo of you smiling without it. They will take a photo without a smile, a left profile photo, a right profile photo, a full body photo and possibly a candid photo aka personality photo.

Here is the **key** to the **no smile photo**, *don't stare into the camera lens like a dead fish. Bite down on your teeth lightly and squint your eyes just a tad bit to give your face a little character.* You want your no smile photo also to tell a story.

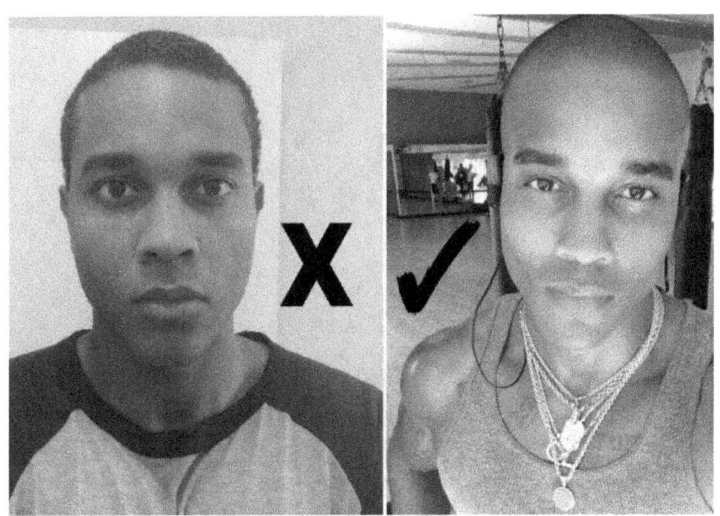

Here is the **key** to the **profile photos**, when facing left or right, use your side smile very lightly. Visualize something pleasant. You don't want the smile to be too noticeable. If casting says, no smile, then bite down on your teeth very lightly and visualize a mark on the wall. You want to give your profile photos some character as well.

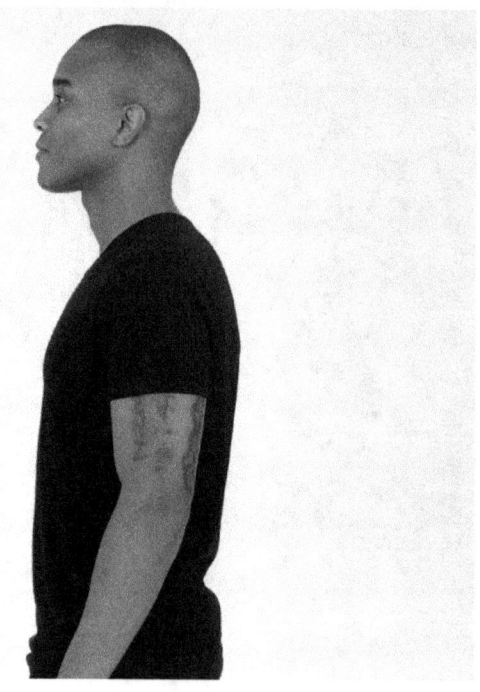

Here is the **key** to the **full body photo**; they are going to ask you to duplicate the smiling photo or the no smile photo showing your whole body. There are several options you can use with this. You can put more weight on one foot than the other, one hand in a pocket with the thumb slightly out, with the pressure on the same foot as the pocket with the hand in it, or you can stand straight up. Utilize the advice about the smile and no smile expressions.

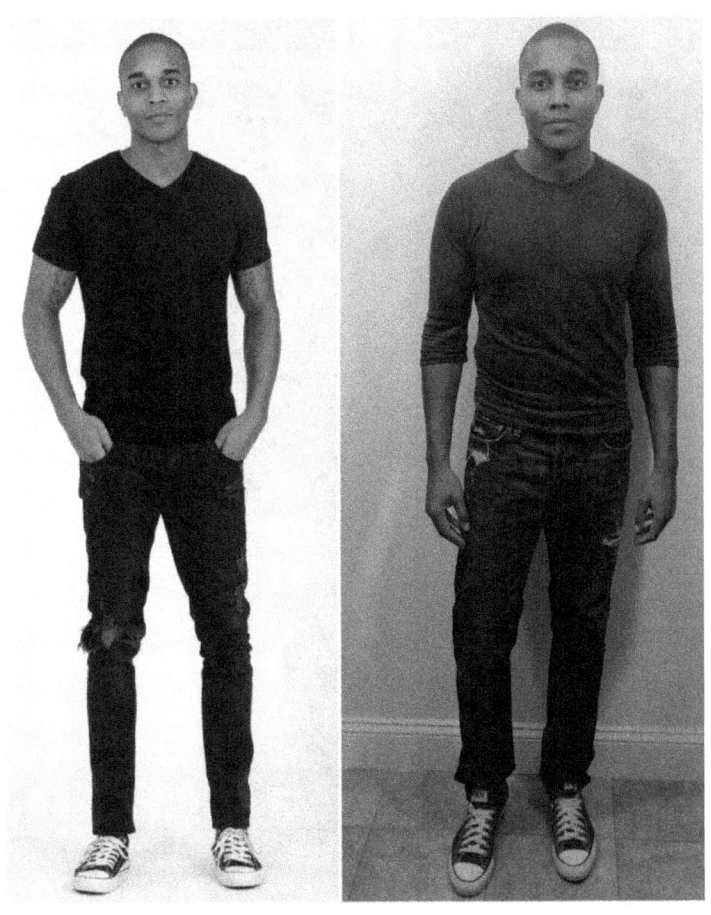

Here is the **key** to the **candid photo a.k.a the personality photo**; be as big as you want to be. Showcase any funny poses that you've been withholding. Duplicate all of the silly poses from the pictures that you take with your friends. Do the rock stars pose with your tongue out. Do weird positional poses, light jumps, laugh really big, etc. Do anything that shows a different side of you that is silly, funny, cute, edgy, creative and likable.

THE MACTOR'S GUIDE

Practice these poses in the mirror until you have mastered them. Add your own personality to it, and when the time arises, you'll be ready.

TONGUE TWISTERS

We all suffer from being tongue-tied. Nervousness is one factor that causes it. This happened to me on several occasions. One reason is that I was raised in the southern part of the United States. I have what is considered a southern accent. I pronounce some words differently and blend many words together as if it was one word.

An example would be Boomhauer from the cartoon TV show "King of the Hill" or listen to any of the Entertainment celebrities from various parts of the Southern United States to get an idea. In any case, we all suffer from the matter of getting tongue-tied while reading scripts out loud during a performance. While I was in Cape Town, South Africa for modeling, I had the opportunity to train some models to help our agency book more jobs as a unit. In doing so, the owner gave us some tongue twisters to help with getting tongue-tied. There are two that stuck with me, and I use them before I practice or before walking into an audition to help clear up my speech.

"Eleven benevolent elephants"

"Red leather Yellow leather"

Before every audition, drink a glass of water, gargle, and spit it out in the sink. Then, stretch your tongue by sticking it straight out as far as you can and lift, up, down, left and right. Repeat the tongue twisters several times. Start off slow and then say them quickly. Once you're done, read your script out loud. You should notice a difference.

STRETCH BEFORE THE AUDITION

It's natural to feel nervous and tense before an audition. Find an area and stretch before going into the audition room. Stretching calms the body down, allowing you to be loose. Sometime auditions require physical activities. Not all auditions are just going to have you stand there and talk.

READ OUT LOUD AND TO YOURSELF

When you receive a commercial or theatrical script, read it out loud and practice while looking in the mirror. You need to listen to how you sound and know how you look when you're delivering the lines. If you believe the style of your voice when you say the lines and how you look, then everyone else will. I've done this several times, to get an idea of what I look like when delivering lines.

MASTERING THE COLD READ

Sometimes at an audition, you'll receive a random script to learn before entering the room. I know that it can be nerve-wracking. I will tell you how to overcome that. First things first, calm down and breathe. Casting isn't expecting you to be perfect. They want to see what you're able to do with short notice. They also do this to see a ***natural performance*** because Mactors usually have a script for more than two days, so their performances are rehearsed.

First Key: For ***commercial*** auditions, *deliver the first line directly to the camera, then glance down at the paper to find the next lines and then look up and give them.*

For ***theatrical*** auditions, *repeat the first step but read directly to the reader instead of the camera. Before you glance down at the paper to read your next line, maintain eye contact with the reader until they have finished delivering their lines. Then, glance down and find your place to provide your following lines to the reader.*

Second Key: *Deliver the last line directly to the camera if it's commercial and straight to the reader if it is theatrical.*

Practice this method on your downtime to become familiar with it. I have used this method, and it landed me a producer session in South Africa for a television show.

DANCE EVEN IF YOU'RE TERRIBLE

Some auditions will ask you to dance. Don't be afraid to dance in front of the camera. Casting directors and their clients could care less if you're a professional dancer. If casting wanted professional dancers, they would request them. They only want to see if you're willing to let loose and have a great time doing it.

Go for it!! I've witnessed people who were terrible dancers in auditions book national TV commercials. They're getting paid a lot of money, especially if it's a SAG project. In 2012, I had a commercial print audition for Bacardi. When I went into the room, casting said that they wanted to see me dance. The scenario was a party scene. I was excited because I can actually dance.

They turned the music on, and I gave them my best 70's John Travolta "Saturday Night Fever" dance moves, diddy bop moves, electric slide, and other various dance moves. I really let loose. I was laughing and having a good time. I booked that commercial print job for Bacardi, and it paid $7500.00 for one day of work.

Now let me ask, are you afraid to dance if it's a possibility that you'll make $7,500.00? You better dance even if you have two left feet. You'll thank me later when you book that job. I also practice dancing terribly or silly because sometimes being too talented at dancing will eliminate you. Sometimes they want to see the humor in your dancing, and there is nothing funny about a great dancer.

TALK ABOUT SOMETHING FOR A MINUTE

Sometimes at auditions, the casting director will ask you questions like, what is your favorite food, place to eat, hobby, etc. Practice talking about these topics for 1 minute. It's better for the casting director to stop you from talking than for you not to have much to say. Casting can't see your personality if they ask; "*Hey Benz, what is your favorite food and why?*" and I reply with; "*steak and because it tastes good.*" That audition tape will probably be deleted as soon as you leave the room. Don't be that person. **PRACTICE!!**

HEAD SHOTS

Headshots are critical. Headshots will determine if you will be requested for an audition. One of my theatrical agents informed me that the floating head photos aren't the standard anymore. The clients want to see more of your body now. Take pictures that are from the abdomen to chest up to show more of your body.

CHARACTER HEADSHOTS

Only shoot character headshots if you're committed to the character. It's risky to photograph these types of photos because they can look unnatural. Clients typically want to see if you have the look of the character without the uniform. However, if you look great in the costume and feel that you can pull off the look, shoot with the outfits. It may put you ahead in the selection process.

EMBRACE YOUR WOW FACTOR

Your **WOW** factor is basically, the ability to charm an individual. It happens typically between two opposite sexes. For example; one day I was eating at a buffet restaurant, and I wanted some avocado rolls made since they didn't have them available. I politely asked the male sushi maker could he make them. He wouldn't make the rolls. I went back to my seat upset and hungry. The young lady that I was with decided to approach the man and ask if he could make the avocado rolls. He didn't make the rolls, but he gave her the ingredients to make them at the table.

The presence of a woman had softened him up to cooperate versus doing nothing for me. The same notion applies in the audition rooms. When I go into an audition room, I immediately look for a woman casting director. If she is present, I start working my **WOW** factor. I use my boyish smile, light-hearted jokes, etc. This is used to give off tremendous positive energy in the room. Once you've won the casting director over, they will fight for you to go to the next level, which is the callback.

The call back is where the clients are in the room. It's usually male-dominated. However, sometimes there are one to two women in the crew. That is who I work my **WOW** factor on. I make sure I make eye contact with them, work the boyish smile, and charm them upon entering the room and when I leave. When they go back and deliberate, I will now have the casting director and the women fighting on my behalf.

This same strategy also works for women. You have to be a little careful not to give off being too flirty. Give off a likable girl next door *WOW* factor.

Practice your *WOW* factor on small things like a discount on merchandise at stores, obtaining extra food, trying to skip the club lines, etc. The *WOW* factor is used in everyday life. Once you master it, it will work for you in an audition.

AUDITION CLOTHES

When it comes to auditioning clothes, I buy clothes that I like and would wear in public. It gives me options and more use out of my clothes. I can wear them to auditions and on set when production requests us to bring clothing options. I can only give the male perspective on specific attire. The following is a list of clothing that all **male** Mactors should have in their wardrobe:

- Black V or Crew neck T- shirt
- Gray V or Crew neck T- shirt
- Black button up shirt
- Dark blue button up shirt
- Light blue button up shirt (commercial)
- White button up shirt
- Black and brown reversible belt
- Black dress shoes
- Brown dress shoes
- Blue and white converse (Chuck Taylors)
- Solid Black converse (Chuck Taylors)
- Slim fit brown Khakis

- Slim fit blue jeans (no rips or distressed)
- Slim fit black jeans (no rips or distressed)
- One suit (preferably black)
- Alternate color suit jacket (preferably burgundy or maroon)
- Black slim fit dress pants (if you bought a different suit)
- Black tie (preferably skinny tie)
- Cardigan sweater
- Vest (black or gray)
- Dress socks
- Boxer briefs (no brand if possible)
- Athletic attire (no brand if possible)
- Swimming trunks
- Brown boat shoes
- Brown flip flops

I have all of these items, and they have helped me book numerous jobs. While on set one day, a young man didn't bring any clothes when previously asked to do so by production. When the wardrobe stylist asked why he said that he doesn't wear any of the clothes that they asked him to bring. The lady gave him a serious lecture. She let him know that if he was serious about having a career in this industry, he needs to buy some clothes.

Now that you have the list of essentials, you will be ahead of the curve on auditions and have the clothes to take to set after you book some work. ***Ladies***, your list varies as you have so many options. However, you can apply some clothing off of the men's list to yours such as; t-shirts, athletic wear, cardigans, converse, etc.

GROUP AUDITIONS

There will be times that you will be placed in groups at auditions. The client may want to book couples or a group of friends. This can be challenging, especially if you aren't used to talking to strangers. I will share with you some pointers that I've learned and used to help book these types of auditions.

Never look directly into the camera during the scenario. You should turn your face towards the camera. Imagine that someone is out past the camera and you acknowledge them.

Never turn your back to the camera or cover someone else up from the camera. If casting's camera can't see your face, then you may not get picked.

Always have stories even if you have to make them up. Practice telling these stories. I have been in auditions and created accounts randomly. Many Mactors have been the guy who had a car that they put a muffler on it to make it sound like a motorcycle but instead, it made their car sound like a lawnmower. Then they picked me up from a girl's house and embarrassed me. I give women Mactors weird boyfriends and ask are they still together? Of course, the stories were created, but it received laughs out of the Mactors, casting directors and landed me jobs.

Go all the way but ask first. Sometimes in group auditions, the scene will call for you to be a real couple. Sometimes it will imply that a kiss can happen. Go for the kiss but ask your partner first. No tongue action is needed. A simple peck on the lips will solidify that you're a real couple.

If the other Mactors in the group isn't acknowledging you in the scene, don't worry. Always stay attentive and keep talking. Also, you can turn your face towards the camera as if you're conversing with an imaginary friend. It doesn't matter if they acknowledge your real conversation because casting is looking at your facial expression, body language, and atmosphere.

Don't try to outshine your group, just be in the moment naturally like as if you were with your real friends. If you decide to be a camera hog, casting will notice, and you likely won't book the job.

Utilize these pointers when you have group auditions. I have booked plenty of commercials and print jobs following these simple instructions. Group auditions are very enjoyable, and it gives you the opportunity to meet some new people and work on your people skills.

SMILE, IT'S NOT ALWAYS ABOUT YOU
BUT THEN AGAIN, IT IS.

It's important to smile and be friendly when you introduce yourself to the camera. However, when you're in the room with other Mactors, **REMAIN SMILING!** After introducing yourself, keep a soft smile on your face when others are introducing themselves.

Stay engaged to what they are talking about because sometimes the camera shows a little of you. It's embarrassing when the cameraman is interviewing another

Mactor, and they can see your face off to the side with disinterest.

ALWAYS BRING YOUR SCRIPT

In 2012, I had an audition for the TV show "The Game" for the character Blue on BET television network. At that time, I was the new face on the scene and was booking jobs left and right. I felt that no matter what I auditioned for, I was going to book it. I wanted to act, and my agent believed that I had the raw talent for performing as well.

I had taken an acting class back in 2011 in Boston before moving to LA, but that wasn't enough. The only thing I knew how to do was repeat the lines over and over. I read the lines out loud, recorded them, and I listened to them for two days. I knew the entire script verbatim. I felt extremely confident. When I arrived at the studio, I put the script in my book bag. After signing in, I sat outside until it was my turn. I didn't want to see the other talent or hear their performance. While waiting, I listened to the lines over and over through my headphones.

When my name was called, I took my headphones off and turned my game face on. I went into the room, the woman was somewhat seated on the office desk. There wasn't a camera in the room. She introduced herself, and she started asking me routine questions. The cordial conversation confused me because I had never experienced that before. After we finished talking, she asked me if I was ready. I responded with yes, and she said; "ok, let's begin."

She looked at me as if she was waiting for me to say something. In that instance, I forgot that I start the conversation in the script. My mind went blank, and I didn't remember anything that I was repeating for the past two days. The lady became aggravated and asked where my script was. I told her that it was in my book bag. After I retrieved my script, I completed the session. She gave some very constructive criticism.

She stated that I needed to enroll in an acting class. She said that she could tell that I was a beginner but not to worry because I have a look that will book some roles. She said that I wasn't ready for this role yet, but she will definitely see me again. I was so embarrassed but accepted what she said. It inspired me like never before. I immediately called my agent and told him what happened.

I made a vow never to let that happen again. Shortly after that, I signed up for acting school. That's when I learned never to be too confident to neglect your script. Your script is your best friend. Casting doesn't want to see a completed character in the audition. When you hold a script, it shows that you still have room to take a different direction from the director.

HOLDING THE SCRIPT

Hold the script by your side, in front of you and with one hand. Your elbow should be bent at around your waistline. This way, you keep the script away from your face. It also allows you to make eye contact with the person that you're reading with behind the camera. Never hold it with two hands. It's difficult to hide your nervousness if you're holding the script with two hands. It will shake a lot, causing a distraction. You don't want to appear nervous in an audition room. Practice in the mirror holding the script as suggested.

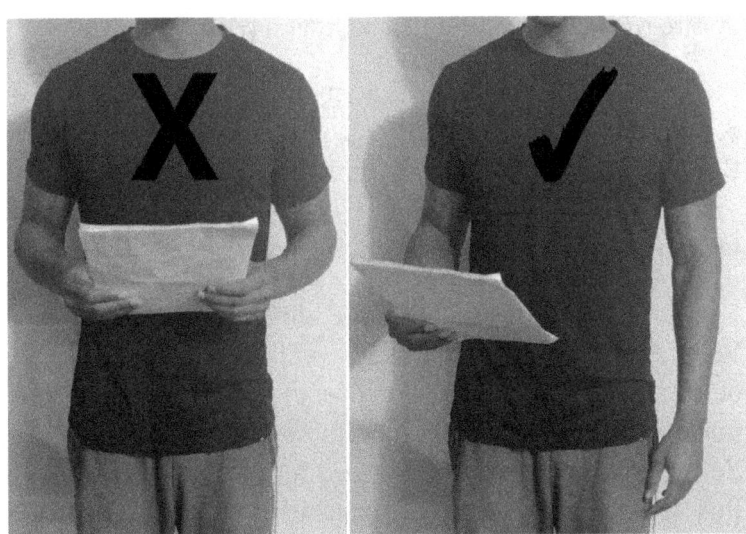

PAY ATTENTION TO DETAIL
FIND THE COMMONALITY

Commonality. *n. a sharing of features or characteristics in common; possession or manifestation of common attributes. (Dictionary.com)*

When you first walk into an audition room, pay close attention to everything in there. In anyone's space, whether work or home, they tend to put things in there that reflects who they are. Find a commonality for you to use. If the casting director has on a Philadelphia Eagles shirt, then you're a Philadelphia Eagles fan that day.

Pay attention to anything that can be a conversation starter and make you memorable and likable. Remember, once a casting director likes you, they will request you for more auditions. They will also fight for you to get picked for more jobs.

In 2017, I auditioned for the movie "I Feel Pretty." In the first audition, I went in for two roles; the cute guy and cute dude. For one of them, the scene took place in a pharmacy store, and the other one took place in Soul Cycle. When I arrived, I read for the Cute Guy role. In this scene, I was a guy trying to flirt with a woman in a pharmacy. I did well, and they requested me for a call back session.

THE MACTOR'S GUIDE

I Feel Pretty Callback Inbox

Tim Ayers
to me
6/19/2017 View details

Hi Benz!

You have a callback for the I Feel Pretty movie!

It's going to be this Friday, June 23rd at Boston Casting.

For the role of Cute Guy at 2:00pm.

Anna will be back in the office tomorrow and will be able to answer any questions that you may have regarding this.

Thank you!

I came into the room greeting everyone with a smile. I went in front of the camera and stood on my mark. The casting director started telling the director that I was from LA and had just returned to Boston. The director said that he was from LA too. **BINGO!!!** The commonality was found. We started talking about where we lived in LA. I lived in Hollywood and he lived in Hollywood. We actually lived right around the corner from each other. So after a few minutes of talking about our experiences in Hollywood, we began the scene. I read for the "Cute Guy" role again. After I finished the audition, I left with a smile on my face. I didn't hear anything about the job, so I figured I didn't book it.

One day I received an email from my agent saying that I booked the movie part. However, it was for the other role that I didn't audition for. The character I booked was "Cute Dude." I was a little confused but still happy that I booked a movie role with a speaking part.

Someone can say that I booked the role because I auditioned well and that may be true. However, I auditioned for a different character altogether. Therefore, someone can say that I booked the role because the casting director liked me, a commonality was found between the director and me, and the "Cute Dude" role was given to me because of it. Practice paying attention to detail and finding commonality among strangers. It will help you at auditions.

DON'T HAND AND HEAD ACT

In real life, we are very animated in how we express ourselves. We talk with our hands and move our heads during a conversation. It is hard to stay focused on what the individual is saying because we are too busy following their hands and head movements.

This doesn't work for TV and film acting. Sometimes the camera shots are so close when filming that the camera lens can't handle all of that movement. Imagine how the audience will feel watching you. Learn to convey your emotions with as little movement of your head and hands as possible.

Theater Acting is a whole different story. You can bring more personality on stage. You have to perform big enough for the audience to hear and see what you're trying to convey. If you go into an audition hand and head acting for TV and film, the casting director will know that you're still a novice and need training. You may not get called in for them again.

ESTABLISH SOME BASICS

IN THE SCRIPT

When you first receive the script, there are some basic things that you should establish.

What is going on in the scene: Search for what's really going on? *Is it an argument? Is it a breakup?* It is essential to know.

The Why: After you figure out what's going on in the scene, ask why it's happening or why did it happen? *It's an argument that led to a breakup because you were caught cheating.*

What is your relationship with the other characters: After you find out why the scene is happening, ask yourself what your relationship with them is. What's the back story? If one isn't available, create one. Are you friends, co-workers? Are they your boss, teacher? Etc. "*We have been together in a committed relationship for five years, since college. We've had ups and downs, but she is my first love*". It is essential to know the relationship and back story because it will guide your responses in the scene.

These are a few basics that I use when I see a script for the first time. If you have never taken an acting class, these three questions will help you get started.

BE THE CHARACTER

There is always an argument about which acting method is the best. Everyone has different ways of learning and applying what they've learned. Personally, I am a fan of method acting. Ask yourself this; is it better to pretend to be a character that isn't really a part of who you are at an audition or practice being the character for a few days before going into an audition? Now I'm not saying go out, and smoke crack to portray a crack head, but I will suggest hanging around one in their environment to understand them better. You should watch their mannerisms, talk to them, etc.

If an audition calls for being a jock, then be a jock in real life. Become a nerd for a day or two, learn the lingo and how to hack. Try characters out and have fun with it. If you are in the audience and someone came to speak to you about your problems but never experienced them, would you listen to them? Or would you rather listen to the person who has been where you've been? It's difficult to believe someone who is portraying a gangster that has never participated in any gangster activities versus an ex-gangster who became an actor.

REPETITION IS THE FATHER OF LEARNING

When you obtain your script, one of the first things you want to do is memorize the lines. Repeat the lines over and over but without doing any acting. I like to learn the script page by page. Repeat page one at least three times and on the fourth time, say the lines without looking at the script. Once that is accomplished, move on to page two. Repeat the same process until you finish the whole script and it is memorized. Then start reading through the entire script from beginning to the end without looking at the text. During the process of repeating each page three times, change the tempo of reading the lines.

Practice this method, and you'll know your lines in no time. It will free your mind to have fun in the audition room because you wouldn't have to depend on looking at the script frequently to find the next line.

BOOKS ON YOUR HEAD I SAID

At runway show auditions, they'll have you walk the runway for them. I walk with a book on my head before any runway audition. The book aids in helping your posture and balance as you are walking. You can't walk on your toes, wobble or in an uneven pattern because the book will fall off.

Whatever the problem is with your walking, the book will let you know. I walk on my toes regularly, so this exercise helps me before I go into a runway audition.

Here's what you do;

Grab a book (preferably a hardback book) and place it on top of your head.

Go to one side of a room or stand at the end of a hallway. I usually practice in my room, but a corridor works as well.

Walk twenty steps from where you started, stop, turn around and return back to your starting point. That is considered one time.

Do this exercise five times for a total of three sets. Do this before bedtime and in the morning before you go to your audition. I used to do this exercise to the point that I could walk around the house all day with a book on my head and do other activities without it falling off.

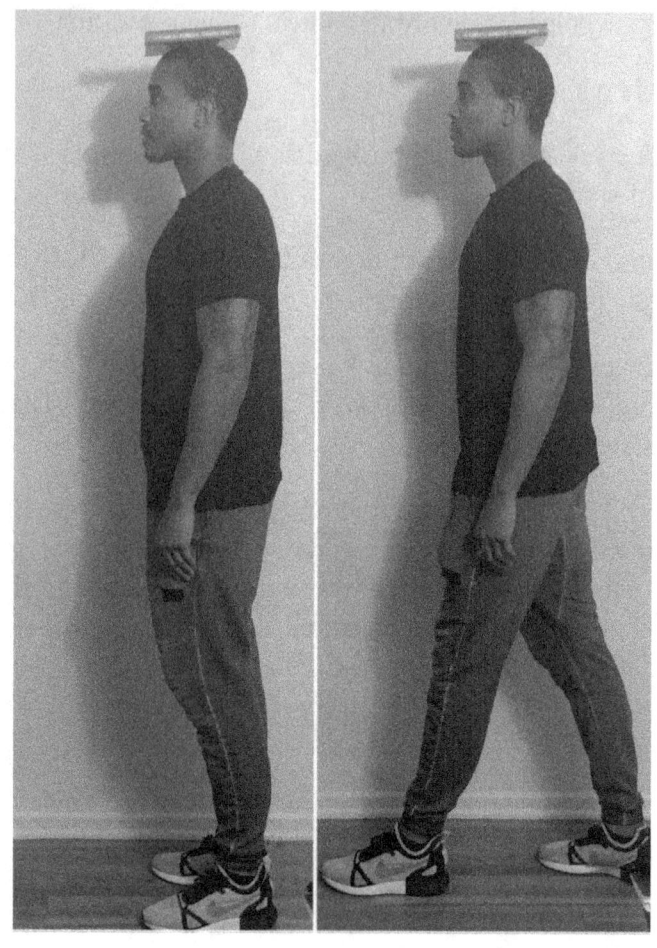

Chapter 3

HOW TO SURVIVE MODELING AND ACTING FULL TIME

In this section of the book, I will be going over some of my journey as a Mactor. I have been modeling and acting full time for seven years and counting. So, it is only right that I share some of my experiences. I will give advice on what you should and shouldn't do to survive in this business. I will go over some of my triumphs and some of the mistakes that you should avoid. So let's get started.

ACQUIRE WOMEN FRIENDS

Most of my life has been predicated on obtaining female friends. Why? Like a mother, they have a nurturing spirit. That means if they really like you whether friendship or intimate, they will naturally care about your well being. They won't allow you to be homeless or without food.

When I decided to take the plunge into this career and move out to Hollywood, CA in 2011, the first thing I wanted to do is find a place to live. At the time, I told myself that I had $2000.00 to invest in finding an apartment. So I began searching online through various websites. I befriended one of my cast mates from the reality TV show we were previously on.

I expressed that I wanted to move out to California and pursue being a full-time model and actor. She offered that I could stay with her at no cost. I was a little reluctant at first, but as I grew impatient searching for a place, I finally took her up on her offer. So the $2000.00 that I was going to spend on finding a place to live ended up being used to invest in my career.

When my time was up living with the castmate, I was faced with a situation of having to return back to Boston. Luckily, I had acquired a new female friend who opened up her home to me so I wouldn't have to end my career early. At that time I had only booked one modeling print job in LA, and the check didn't come yet.

In the summer of 2012, I started my bicoastal run as a Mactor. I had acquired a woman friend from one of the seasons of "Bad Girls Club." She opened up her doors for me to live so I could model and act in New York for the two months that I was going to be there. I booked two jobs while I was there.

What if I never acquired any female friends? Where would I have been? Probably still in Boston trying to figure it out. If you're a woman reading this book, the same applies. Throughout my career, I have met many women who have shared stories of letting their girlfriends stay at their place with no job, money, etc. some male friends will offer you their couch to sleep on if you need it and I have some of them too. It is essential that you are **GENUINE** with your friendship. I am a genuine friend to these people. If they ever call me in need of something and I'm able to do it, I will. As long you are being a good friend, that bridge will never be burned between you two.

DON'T DEPEND ON AGENTS

SIGN UP FOR CASTING SITES

Signing up for casting websites is essential to surviving. Not only can you be discovered on them, but you can also book work. When I first got to LA, I signed up for LA casting and Actors Access. Sometimes you can score big on these sites. I have booked jobs on these sites.

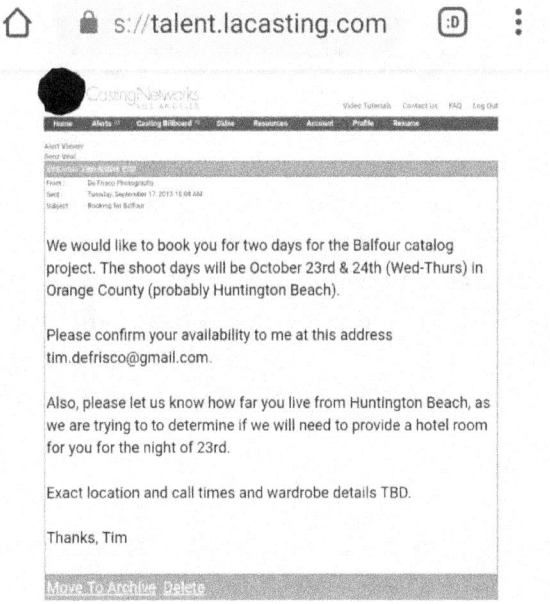

If you have an agent, understand that they are busy. They have hundreds of models and actors to tend to. If you aren't on their favorites list or booking frequently, then you aren't a priority to them. However, you're a priority to yourself.

KEEP A LOW OVERHEAD

Use Public Transportation: This is a no brainer for anyone in the New York City Market. The majority of the population in New York City uses public transportation. This is for Mactors who are in Los Angeles, CA. For the first 3 years of my career in LA, I utilized public transit. My goal was to find an apartment that is centralized to where the auditions would be held. I needed to live near a bus stop. When you're modeling and acting full time, public transportation is your best friend. You can multi-task while the bus driver is stressed about being traffic. You can also learn about the city at the same time.

There is a negative stigma about riding the bus and train in LA. One evening I was at a comedy show, and a comic was talking about how everyone in LA drives and thinks that everyone who rides the bus is poor. Sometimes your social life will suffer because people will grow tired of picking you up to go to events. It's difficult to hang out late because the train and bus stop running at a particular time.

Don't worry about these people because you're there for work and not pleasure. When I first started riding public transportation in 2011, it cost me $75.00 a month. The price has increased over the years. Now, would you rather pay that monthly or pay close to $75.00 a week in gas, be stuck in traffic and encounter expensive parking tickets? Don't ride the bus and train at night ladies. Utilize Uber, Lyft and the taxi. The object of public transportation is to save money.

Home cook meals are the way to go: Eating out becomes expensive if you're eating out on the regular. It is ok to treat yourself to a luxury meal every once in a while. I was like a robot. My first roommates in Los Angeles, CA thought that I only ingested smoothies, grilled chicken breast, and oatmeal every day. The truth is, that's what I ate every single day. Grocery shopping for me was very inexpensive and kept my overhead low.

When I was in South Africa for work, I cooked a lot of my food. I was able to eat out a little more there because the American dollar is stronger than their money. I suggest that you find a system of food that you don't mind eating every day and stick to that. I know this can be difficult, but try it out. I still follow this system of cooking my own food, eating the same type of food every day and rarely eating out.

Party sparingly, when it's free or inexpensive: Going out to the club frequently can deplete your finances quickly. Women have it easy in this department because they usually gain access to establishments for free. Men are always offering to buy them drinks as well. When I hung out with certain celebrities or political friends, I didn't have to pay for entry to clubs or beverages, whether alcoholic or non-alcoholic.

I chose bars and lounges over clubs because there wasn't a cover charge. Also in these establishments, the drink prices are more affordable. There was a place in Los Angeles that I would visit on some Tuesdays. I went to this place because on Tuesdays, they had $2 slushy drinks and $1 bar appetizers. So you could get inebriated and eat food for $6 and go home.

Imagine this; the club's cover charge is roughly $20, now add two drinks at $14 to start out. You've invested $48 and probably not even buzzed. You see a girl that you're interested in, so you buy both of you a drink. Now you've invested $76, and that's without tipping. You can save a little if you get a beer instead. Imagine if you went out once every weekend like that.

That is around $304 a month. That is $3,648.00 a year. That isn't a wise investment if you want to survive as a Mactor full time. I rarely go out partying, but when I do, it is free entry or $10. I usually drink $2 Shirley temples (sprite or ginger ale and grenadine).

Find affordable housing: Many Mactors think they have to rent a very nice apartment to live in. Sometimes up to 4 people live in a tiny 1 bedroom or studio apartment. Don't be ashamed to stay somewhere less desirable to save money and have peace of mind. When I found my first place to live, it wasn't the most luxurious location, but the bathroom and kitchen were clean. I had my own room, and I was paying $475 a month including utilities.

I knew Mactors who paid more than me and shared a room because they wanted to live in Hollywood, West Hollywood, North Hollywood, Beverly Hills, etc. They didn't have the privacy or the peace of mind that I had. Ladies, I understand that security is a vital importance to you, so I suggest choosing a place affordable as possible but satisfies your safety needs.

It's ok to couch surf: This is a great temporary option to save some money. Couch surfing is sleeping on someone's couch for free or for a lower price than the market rent. Before you stay your first night, plan your exit strategy. Don't be ashamed to do this, this is normal for Mactors. I did it before in 2012. When I returned to Los Angeles, CA, I couched surf on a sofa bed for almost two weeks before I found my first apartment. A female friend of a political friend of mine let me stay there.

Sometimes you have to dog sit: You save money, and you have a place to live. Sometimes I had to dog sit for a few days to a week when my friend was out of town for business.

Buy what's necessary & nothing more: When you go grocery shopping, buy what you need for consumption for that day or the next few days. Don't buy anything that you would end up throwing away because it's just sitting in the cabinet. The only items that should be sitting in your kitchen cabinets are seasonings and possibly can goods. This strategy eliminates a lot of money being wasted on buying additional food.

BUY A CAR, PILLOW & A BLANKET

Many will say; "of course buy a car Benz, duh." However, my reasons for buying a car have a different perspective. Yes, a car is needed in certain markets like Atlanta and Boston to get to your auditions. I say buy a car because you may have to live in your car at some point in your career.

It's nothing to be ashamed of. I have personally lived in my car for two months before. I had returned from Africa in 2014, and I was only going to be in LA for two months. It didn't make sense for me to pay for a room or hotel for two months. I decided to live out of my car, and I would shower at the gym. I would cut my hair at a friend's house. You can also use the gym to cut your hair.

Many people who have made it in this industry have slept in their car. Tyler Perry, Steve Harvey just to name a couple. This is normal for Mactors. You can't be afraid to do this or have this logic of thinking. Of course, this is for emergencies only, but it is great to have this plan B.

BUY YOUR OWN EQUIPMENT

Being self-sufficient is great. The acting industry requires a lot of self-tape auditions. I bought video cameras, lights, backdrops, and tripods because you can't always access a self-tape business. However, if you have your own equipment, you don't have to depend on them.

ACQUIRE OTHER SKILLS

If you want to survive in this industry, you are going to have to learn other skills. You can't always wait for people when it's about your career.

Learn how to edit your own photos: You will deal with photographers that will only give you a limited amount of edited images and leave you with a lot of raw, unedited photos. They will offer to charge you more money to edit the other ones. Sometimes you and the agency may not have the same taste in pictures for the photographer to edit.

I ran into this problem and decided to learn how to do it myself. I spent some time in Adobe Photoshop. I looked at how some of my edited photos looked and tried to mimic the look. I would listen to what agents would say about the type of photos they were looking for as far as edits. Sometimes edited photos look too perfect and unrealistic so I would edit them to look more real with a light clean up. Make Adobe Photoshop your best friend, and you will never have to deal with waiting for a photographer for edits.

Learn to create your own acting reel: You will need an acting reel. The acting reel is your visual resume. It is a testament to your acting work. This can lead to obtaining more acting work. When I wanted to put an acting reel together finally, I began searching for places that offer this service. After looking up a few places, I saw how expensive it was.

I started thinking of a way to do it myself. I stumbled across an application on my laptop called Windows Movie Maker. I started adding videos to it and trimming the videos for the parts that I wanted. After hours of using with it, I became a pro at using movie maker and creating acting reels. Anytime I need to edit my reel, I don't have to pay someone. Take some time and learn how to use Movie Maker, iMovie or whatever video editing app you like.

Learn to write your own contracts: After I was on the Reality TV show, I started hosting parties at clubs. I became my personal manager and wrote up contracts to give to the club promoters. I looked at some contracts that my reality TV star colleagues had used with promoters and learned how to write them myself.

AVOID PERPETUITY

Sometimes you will be presented with a contract that may have the term "***perpetuity***" in it. You want to avoid signing that contract unless you **really need** the money.

Perpetuity: *n. 1. The state or quality of lasting forever. 2. A bond or other security with no fixed maturity date - (oxford dictionary)*

This means that if you sign a contract with perpetuity in it, the company can use your image forever. Even when you are old, they can use your young image and never have to pay you outside of the initial payment. They will make millions off of you in comparison to the pennies they paid you.

I first learned about this term when I became the poster child for American Eagle. I had booked the job in Los Angeles, CA through my New York, NY agency's west coast branch. The LA agency revealed to me that the contract was a bad one because perpetuity was in the contract and explained to me what it meant. How would you feel if 10 years later, a company was still using your face making millions, and you were only paid $400? Be Cautious with your image.

SIGN NON EXCLUSIVE UNTIL THEY EARN EXCLUSIVITY

You should fight to sign nonexclusive contracts with agencies. I understand if you don't have experience and agencies have to build you from the ground up. However, if you have established yourself already, why would you give away your option to seek work on your own? When you sign exclusively with an agency, which means you can only work if it is through that agency. You can't find work for yourself without paying them commission, and they did none of the work.

When I first started out, I made sure all my contracts were nonexclusive. My argument was that I already had a fan base and I built it myself. NYMMG gave me a nonexclusive contract as that's how they work in general. Bella agency wanted exclusivity, but I wasn't trying to sign that, so they gave me a nonexclusive contract for a year. Within a year, I had booked so much work that when the contract was finished; I felt they earned the right to sign me exclusively for the Los Angeles, CA market.

When you are nonexclusive, you can find work on your own and work with whoever you want. There is a **drawback** to this. Sometimes agencies won't work as hard in submitting you for projects.

Think about this, what if you were dating someone and you knew that you were sharing him/her with five other partners, would you give your all to him/her?

You probably wouldn't. That is how agencies feel when you don't sign exclusive contracts. That is why I said, sign nonexclusive until they earn exclusivity. There is nothing worse than signing exclusive with an agency, and they never find you work. Many Mactors have made this mistake, and they never worked on any campaigns, TV shows, etc. They are just wasting years looking good on an agency's website.

EAT HEALTHY AND FAST 1 DAY A WEEK

Fasting. v. intransitive verb. 1: to abstain from food. 2: to eat sparingly or abstain from some foods. (Webster's dictionary)

Eating a healthy diet is essential to maintaining a long career. By consuming low-fat foods and staying away from processed sugars, unhealthy starches and flours, you look young and healthy longer. Agave and Date sugar are great substitutes. Wild Rice, Kamut, Farro, and Quinoa are great substitutes for white and brown rice.

Pick one day out of the week to fast for 36 hours. It's beneficial for your immune system and soul. Only drink water (Alkaline water preferred).

PREPARATION MEETS OPPORTUNITY

Someone once told me that luck is preparation meets opportunity. In other words, always stay prepared. When the opportunity presents itself, you'll capitalize on it.

From extra to poster child: Some Mactors look at being an extra as a dead end job. I never looked at it that way. I always looked at being an extra as a chance to learn things about the set or an opportunity to become more. As an extra, you still have a chance to get an upgrade to principal pay. This is what happened to me when I booked the American Eagle campaign.

I originally signed the contract to be a featured extra for them. I was still new to the industry, but I also studied American Eagle's previous campaign ads, so I understood the style they like to shoot in. I already knew my angles towards the camera. On set, I knew where to be, not to look directly into the camera and just have a great time. When the opportunity was presented to put a young lady on my shoulder, I embraced it and had the time of my life.

When the campaign finally came out, they decided to make me the poster child. My agent emailed American Eagle and asked for more money, and we received it with no problem. Don't look at being an extra as a dead end street.

"Sometimes you have to drive through the woods at the end of the street to discover the beach beyond."

From a reader to movie role: Sometimes the auditions aren't won in the audition room. This is how I obtained a movie role and became one of the faces on the billboard for the movie "Detroit" directed by Kathryn Bigelow. I originally auditioned for this movie role but never heard anything back about it.

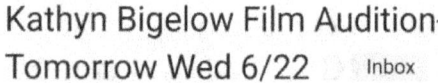

Kathyn Bigelow Film Audition- Tomorrow Wed 6/22   Inbox

 Anna @ Model Club
to
6/21/2016 View details

Hey There!

Details below on an audition at CP Casting for the new Kathryn Bigelow film that Carolyn would like to see you for- it's focused on the Detroit Riots circa 1967- please read the details below and let me know if you can make it/will schedule a time-

This would be a great opportunity to get in for-

Please bring at least 2 Headshots/Resumes-

If booked, this is a SAG project (but would be a great one to be a part of) so please always be aware of your SAG Status (SAG-e, Must-Join, etc)

Audition Date: Wed 6/22
Location: CP Casting- 537 Tremont Street, Boston MA 02116

Role: MIKE
Wardrobe: The Detroit riot time was one of civil unrest and struggle- this film is gritty- *do not* show up really pretty, be natural- plain works- no Boston accents, no

I moved on and focused on the next audition. Time went by, and I received a call from casting. They asked if I would be interested in being a reader for two of the actors that they were trying to choose between. I've never been a reader in this aspect. I've coached actors and rehearsed lines with classmates, but I've never been paid to read for actors.

I agreed to do the job for $100. Immediately after I accepted the job, I said to myself; "I am going to treat this as an audition and really do a great job." I called my dad, told him what had happened and my plan. He agreed with my thoughts.

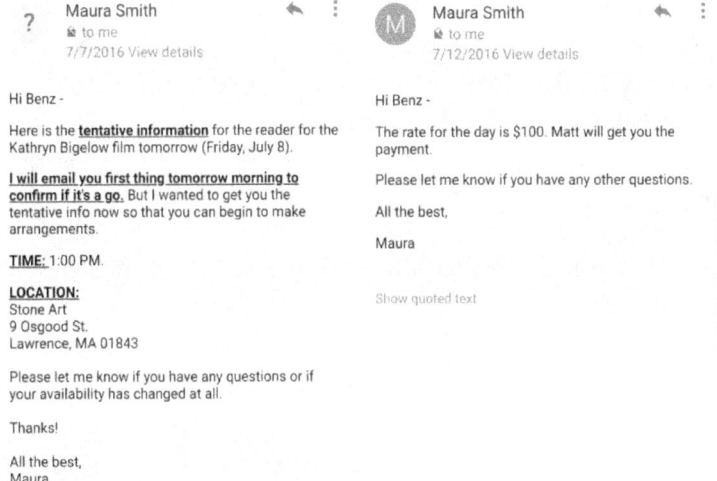

The way I coach and rehearse with Mactors is different. I become the character that they need me to be. I do this to bring the best out of them and because many readers in auditions lack emotions to aid you. On the day when I had to read for the two actors, they brought me to a mock set. They had the real movie cameras there and a production team. This was basically a test for both actors.

I knew that I had to give my best performance to bring out the best from the actors. While they were preparing for everything, I was doing my best to be off book so that I could be fully connected with them. My position was behind the camera, and you could only see the actor that they were auditioning for the role.

The first actor that I read for was pretty good, but I felt like he was holding back. The second actor's performance was better than the previous one, but he held back too. I decided to give more emotion in the next few takes. I put down the script and just acted like I was in the scene with him. I brought so much passion out of him that tears came from his eyes. At that moment I thought to myself; "That's what I wanted to see." After we finished, Kathryn told us a good job, and I went back to my holding area.

While in the holding area, I was telling the other reader which actor I liked. I told her that the second guy was great and I wanted him to get the part. They released us, and I went home. Time went by, and I decided to visit my mom in Charlotte, NC. While I was there, I received a call from casting asking if I could come in to audition for another role for the movie. I told them that I couldn't audition because I was visiting my mom but I could when I return to Boston in a couple of days.

She said ok. After a while, I received another call from casting saying that the director and writer really loved my performance at the read the other day and they wanted to book me. They made a role just for me, and I would be playing a real person. I was overly excited about this. This was my first ever movie role that I actually had a principal role in. When I arrived on set, I saw the young man that I wanted to get the part. I walked up to him and said "congrats man," we chatted and laughed. That young man name is Algee Smith. We both booked a role from that day. Always jump on the opportunity to read for an actor. You never know when it might come in handy.

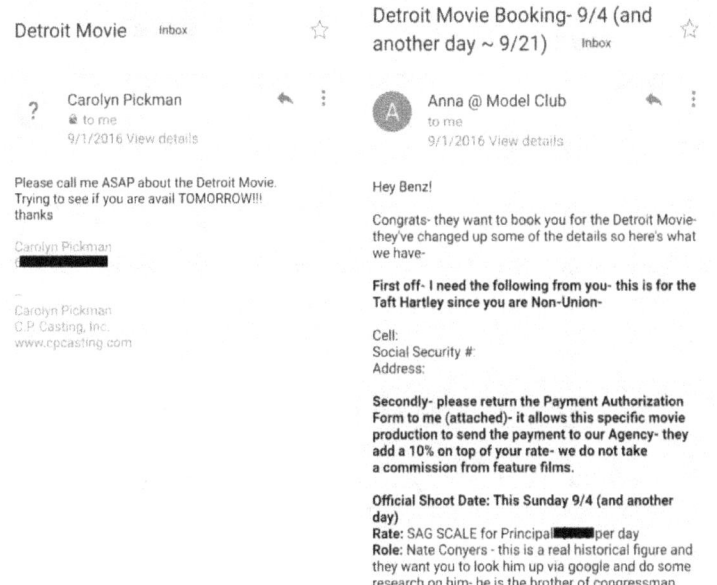

DRUG FREE IS THE WAY TO BE

My dad always preached; "***stay in one state of mind at all times***," so I never used drugs. Using drugs is one way to end your career before it even starts. Drugs will distract you from where you're trying to go in your career, and some people become addicts. I've seen a Mactor that I worked with on a campaign before in the streets looking homeless and strung out. He wasn't signed to the same agency, and I hadn't seen him on any more campaigns for years.

2 DRINK MAX OR DON'T DRINK

I was always taught not to drink and do business. However, in this industry, it's a strong possibility that you may be at a networking event or hanging out with someone who can potentially forward your career. If this ever happens to you, I would suggest that you **don't drink** but as the saying goes; "*It's hard for anyone to trust you, if you don't have a little dirt on you.*" If they are drinkers, they may feel offended if you don't drink with them.

If you choose to drink, I suggest a two-drink maximum and sip slowly. The goal here is to remain coherent but accomplish the networking goal. It's all about being liked in this game.

SAY NO TO NUDE PHOTOS

At the beginning of my career, I was told to never shoot nude with a photographer. It is considered blackmail content, can be leaked out and possibly damage your career. Your naked body is the most valuable asset you have in this industry. Don't just give it up for a free test shoot or small financial gain. People are intrigued by what you may be hiding underneath in hopes that they can get a glimpse. The tease is always better than the reveal. The tease can keep people curious for a long time. Once it's revealed, the curiosity is over, and the interest decreases. For some, if your nudes are leaked, your career will plummet, especially if you aren't already popular and financially stable.

NO TATTOOS

You shouldn't get any tattoos, especially if you're just starting your career as a Mactor. The Industry likes an empty canvas. If they want tattoos on you, they have the technology to put tattoos on you. When I was seventeen, I asked my dad about tattoos, and he said to me; "*No because who knows, you could be a model or actor or something one day.*" I didn't listen because I didn't want to be a model. I wanted to be a night club owner and bail bondsman. I thought I had it all figured out.

Here I am years later, with over twelve tattoos and limited in what I can do in my career. There have only been two jobs that I have booked in my career with all of my tattoos showing in an audition. The two jobs were; The Lady Gaga "Fame" fragrance campaign and the Miller Lite beer print ads. In the Lady Gaga audition, we had to wear a jock strap and dance exotically. They painted our bodies and covered our faces, so you didn't see much of my tattoos. In the Miller Lite audition, I had to take off my shirt and pretend that we were at a beach. I booked that job off of my personality.

After shooting the Miller Lite campaign, it was all laughter and celebration. We started talking about my tattoos, and one of the producers said to me; "*Benz when we saw you with your shirt off, we were like oh my god he has a lot of tattoos, but you had so much personality in your audition tape, that we said; whatever, we will just put a shirt on him*".

There will be some people that will say that tattoos are trending. There are some people in the industry making money with tattoos on their bodies, but not very many. If you are only seeking to model in the urban market, then tattoos are fine. Tattoos are cool and hip and great for conversations. When I am on set, production loves my tattoos. However, my booking percentage is low with my tattoos showing in an audition. The owner of one of my previous agencies said; *"**Benz if you would've arrived at the New York office with your tattoos showing, we wouldn't have signed you."***

If you still decide to get tattoos after this warning, make sure they are small and easy to hide with makeup. If you get arm tattoos, avoid getting any below the elbow or pass your shoulder. Don't get any tattoos that are vulgar, violent or ones that are copyrighted.

EMBRACE BEING THE TOKEN

You ever notice that *ONE* person of color in the group on a print ad, commercial or movie? That person is considered to be the Token. You will hear many people outside of the industry refer to being a token as something negative, but it is not. Being a token in the industry brings vast rewards. You are the go-to person for movies, TV roles, Print ads, etc. What is a token?

Token: *A minority that was deliberately put on a show or movie for the sake of being culturally diverse. (Urban dictionary)*

This doesn't only apply to Minorities. European /Caucasian descent people can be tokens as well.

Eminem is considered a token in the hip hop community as well as Justin Timberlake. They embraced being accepted into the urban culture (people of color's culture) and reap substantial benefits from it. They were in all of the urban magazines, TV shows, etc. In most of my group modeling campaigns, I am usually the only person of color on the campaign ads and sometimes on the set period.

There is high power in being a token. Productions will use you over and over. This means you'll obtain more money and have a longer career. Don't run away from being a token. There is nothing better than standing out among the crowd versus blending in.

DON'T BE A HOMOPHOBE

Homophobe: n. *a person with a dislike of or prejudice against homosexual people. (Oxford Dictionary)*

There is an excellent benefit of being liked by the homosexual community. Someone once said to me; "***Benz you want to be liked by the gays and the straight people.***" In my opinion, once homosexuals like you, the game is almost won. Homosexuals have a strong influence in the entertainment and fashion industry, so you don't want to offend them on a mass level. That is a quick way to end your career.

Homosexual men have complimented me. I accept the compliment and respectfully decline when they try to engage in intimate conversations. I let them know that I am heterosexual and inquire about their beautiful women friends. Always deflect charmingly.

STAY ON THE CASTING DIRECTOR'S RADAR

There are people in this industry called casting directors. They are the individuals you have to see before you are booked on any project. If they like you, they will keep calling you in for various projects that they have to fill for their clients. You want to always remain on their radar. Here are some ways that you can stay in their minds;

Do a great job auditioning: It makes it easier for them to keep calling you in to audition.

Send postcards of upcoming releases: Casting directors are busy and not going to see you on every project. If you have future projects releasing, then send a postcard to keep them aware.

Send a $5 Thank you gift card: Casting directors are always working from morning to night. So coffee is their best friend. If it is your first time auditioning for a casting director, go to your nearest Starbucks and get a $5 gift card and mail it to them in a Colored envelope.

The last two points, I learned in Mike pointers "Hey I saw your commercial" class. They have benefitted me greatly. Not many Mactors are doing this, and you won't regret the investment. There was one casting director in LA that hated my agency but absolutely loved me. She would only call the agency for me to come in and audition for her.

BECOME BI COASTAL & INTERNATIONAL

In my opinion, being a bicoastal talent is the way to be. When my career started flourishing in 2012, my agent suggested that I work in New York because the industry slows down in the summertime in Los Angeles. I went there and booked a few jobs. Visiting New York every summer became my yearly routine.

Being bicoastal was great, but I wanted more. I decided to go international and acquired an agency in Cape Town, South Africa in 2013. I added an agency in Boston, MA in 2015 and in Atlanta, GA in 2018. I added agencies in different states because whenever the market was slow in one city, I could work in another and keep the income and momentum going. The goal is to continue working in your career, not take time off and get a regular job. You have to be mobile, so acquire as many agencies in different cities as possible and take your talents overseas.

SAVE 10% FOR SLOW DAYS

From the moment you start receiving checks from the jobs that you're booking, immediately deduct 10% to save for the slow times in your career. When it rains success, it pours, but when it's slow, it's slower than a snail moving. However, your bills don't stop coming so you will need that money to cover your expenses until the success momentum starts again.

A PRETEND MACTOR BOY/GIRLFRIEND

Some auditions ask for "real" couples. Sometimes casting will pair you up with complete strangers if you don't have a "real partner." I suggest getting a Mactor friend and develop a connection with them. Take photos with them, send them to your agents and upload them on your casting websites. Being in an audition with someone that you already have a natural chemistry with is a great feeling.

I utilized this method before. I called a lady Mactor that I had a previous connection with and asked would she accompany me to an audition as a couple. She agreed, and we both went to NYC and auditioned. We didn't book that particular job, but we were called in for another Job and booked that one. That job was one of the highest paying jobs in my career.

LIVE OFF CREDIT CARDS

When you work on non-union jobs, you usually receive your paychecks within 30-90 days. Most union jobs pay within two weeks. This is why you need a credit card (a high limit card is preferred). With the credit card, you can pay your rent and utilities. You can also cover investments such as; headshots, acting classes, etc. Obtain **cash back**, **flight miles reward**, or **point reward** credit cards. Getting these types of cards put you in a winning situation. For every dollar you spend you will receive cash back, miles for flights or points to use for trips, money, etc.

JOIN SAG OR NOT TO JOIN SAG

This question is always asked, so I will tell you what agents always have told me; "hold off on joining sag for as long as possible." I was SAG eligible for many years, and my career was very lucrative. I was auditioning and working a lot. When I joined SAG, my work and auditions decreased by a great deal.

There isn't as much SAG work versus non-union work. Only join SAG if you have to. In the meantime, enjoy working both non-union and union work. For those who are SAG and thinking of becoming FI-Core because you haven't been working since joining, that is a personal decision. Everyone's path is different. I can say that many actors are becoming FI-Core to be able to work union and non-union jobs. The benefits of a SAG job is the residual income versus being bought out for non-union work. Being bought out means that they only have to pay you one time.

SAG-AFTRA: *Screen Actors Guild - American Federation of Television and Radio Artists*

DO EXTRA WORK SPARINGLY

When you do too much extra work, casting will only see you as an extra. I do extra work when I haven't worked in a while and want to get the ball rolling again, or I want to learn something about the craft. On movie and commercial sets, I like to study how the actors perform. I also learn what directors like, cameras they're using, angles, etc. You can make a living off being an extra on

SAG commercials but if you want to be more than an extra, don't do too much extra work.

MAKE YOUR ONLINE PROFILE LIVE

Upload a video of every talent you possess, acting reel and commercial snippets to these casting websites. Your profile should be as interactive as possible. It will definitely make you stand out more to casting. Pick a new talent, learn it, video record it and upload it to your profile. Agents will ask you to make your profile live because it makes their job easier to submit to clients. When your profile is live, a play button will appear on your resume.

BUILD A RELATIONSHIP WITH YOUR AGENT

Your agents are going to be some of the most important people in your career. Having a great agent is imperative for your survival in this industry. Nurture this relationship like they were one of your closest friends or significant other. You should do some of the same things with your agent that you would do with those types of people. A great agent on your side will fight for you in this industry like your best friend would in real life. Here are some pointers to building a relationship with your agent.

Send $5 coffee gift cards: Agents are on their computers all day and sometimes all night submitting their talent to various jobs. Coffee is their best friend. Implement this strategy after you sign with an agency to give thanks and establish a relationship. Do this periodically when you book a job to give thanks for them working hard for you.

Send holiday gifts and gifts of endearment: Valentine's Day is a great day to send gifts to women agents. Learn about some of the things that your agents like. I had one agent who loved Almonds, so one day I sent him a gift card to buy some almonds. When you show agents that you care about them outside of their job, they will repay the favor with working harder for you in your career. This can range from getting you more auditions to calling in favors to get you free photo shoots.

Always send birthday wishes. Never miss an agent's birthday. Send a birthday wish via text or email. If you are feeling the spirit, send a $5 gift card. They are always appreciated.

Gossip with your agent. You gossip with your friends and relationship partner, so you should do the same thing with your agent. Just like anyone else, agents love to talk to someone, and it's not just about work. I hang out at my agencies sometimes and gossip with them. Hanging out at the agency is equivalent to barbershop and salon talk. You will be liked more, and that turns in to them doing more for you. Sometimes agents call me on the late night, and we chat about whatever is going on in life.

DON'T BECOME TOO ATTACHED TO YOUR AGENT

We've all heard the old saying; ***"all good things come to an end"*** This is true when it comes to your agent. Some agents will retire, quit abruptly, etc. It will leave you in an emotional rut. You became attached to them because y'all working relationship flourished over the years. They leave, and you're left in the hands of agents that are unfamiliar with you.

My career suffered on various occasions with different agencies because of the departure of agents that I had a long term relationship with. I was introduced to new agents frequently that didn't understand how to market me. I started changing agencies hoping to find an agent to duplicate the success that I had with my previous agents. Don't make this mistake. Control your emotions and remember that everything is temporary in life. Build a relationship with every new agent that you encounter.

YOU'RE ALWAYS A LOCAL HIRE

Let your agencies know that you're always a local hire in whatever city your agencies are located. Being a local talent increases your booking chances. If you want to be a local hire in various cities, you have to be willing to *pay for your own flights.* The days of clients paying for Mactor's flights are nearly over. It's not common for lower paying jobs and out of some companies' budgets. That treatment is mostly reserved for high paying jobs.

This is what I tell my agency, "*Any job that wants to book me that is paying $1000.00 and higher, I will pay for my own flight, etc.*"

If you're a big talent, this puts you ahead of the other local talent. Remember you're trying to continue doing this full time. If you're in LA and have to fly to Boston or NYC (I have done this on several occasions) it can range from $200 to 400 roundtrip flight depending on the time frame you have to book your trip. Once you subtract the agency fee which could be $100 to 200, that will leave you anywhere from $400 to 600 profit.

How many people do you know that makes $400 to $600 a day? It's even better if you have a credit card that gives you cash back or flight miles for the purchase.

SOMETIMES YOU HAVE TO TAKE THE LOSS EVEN WHEN YOU CAN WIN

In this industry there are times even though you may be right, you have to be wrong. It's better for you financially and career-wise. Here is a story about how I was ostracized from an agency for being right.

Ostracize: *v. to exclude, by general consent, from society, friendship, conversation, privileges, etc. (Dictionary.com)*

One summer while working on the east coast, I was directly booked for a job in New York. At that time I had two agencies working for me with nonexclusive contracts. I arrived at the job excited because the client was one that I had previously worked for. They were thrilled to have me. I met a model on set that day, and he was a cool guy. We exchanged casual conversation, and then he asked what agency booked me on the job. I told him, and he said that he used to be with that agency too (name dropped some agents), but now he was with the new agency that had booked him for this job. He also signed exclusively with them.

He didn't know that the agency he was signed exclusively with, I was signed nonexclusively with for the New York market. The guy kept bragging about his agency and told me that if I was interested, he could refer me. I told him that I was interested in the North Carolina market because my mom was down there, so it would be cool to have an agency there. He told me that he was signed with an agency there and they only submit for direct bookings with their talent. He said that he could connect me with them. I told him about the Boston market and how I could connect him with an agent there.

After we exchanged contact information, he mentioned his agency again and how he believed that I would be a great fit with them. I told him that I was signed with that agency too. I informed him that I was with that agency since the beginning of my career. We laughed and continued our day on set. The next day, I received an email from our agent asking who had booked me on that job. The guy told the agency about me without knowing the type of relationship I had with them. Two lessons were learned that day;

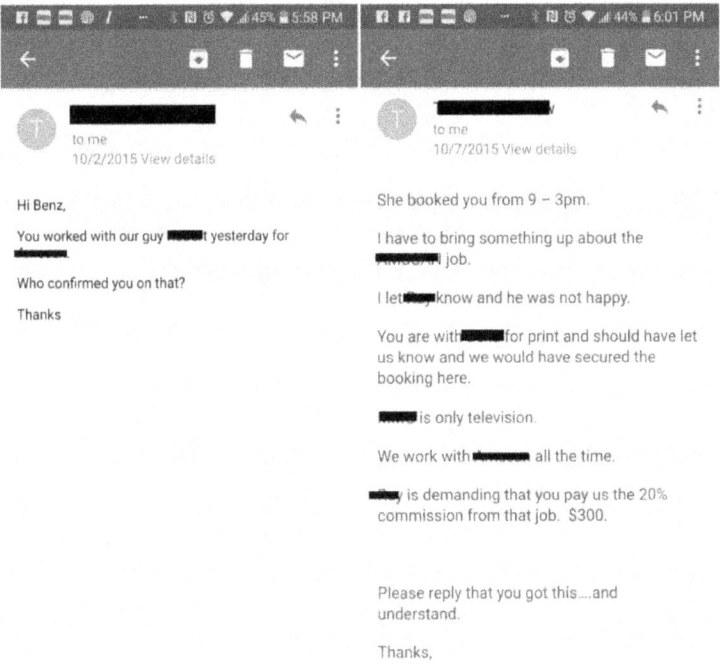

* *Engage in small talk only and keep your business to yourself because all Mactors aren't your friend.*

* *No good deed goes unpunished.*

 The agent explained that he had submitted me to the same job and was wondering why I didn't get called in. I expressed to him that I thought it was odd as well, being that I had worked with that company before through the agency. He emailed that I owed $300.00 for the agency fee for the job. I stated that I didn't owe the money because I was under a non-exclusive contract in New York, so that meant I could work for anyone.

 He said that he would contact the owner because he didn't know the nature of the relationship. The owner reached out to me about the situation and expressed that I was **RIGHT**. He said that since I was signed exclusively in LA, he thought it would carry over to NYC and never considered drawing up another contract for that city. He didn't offer me an exclusive contract, took me off the men's board and put me on the *freelance board*.

 This meant that I wouldn't be working with the same agent that I had built a great working relationship with. I also wouldn't be a priority anymore. I booked one job after that conversation with him as my agent. I went out on a few auditions for the next couple of years before I finally left the agency. I was ostracized for $300.00 that I rightfully didn't owe. However, because he had the power and I depended on them to find me work, he attacked me financially. No more auditions meant, no more money, which could lead to my career possibly ending.

THE MACTOR'S GUIDE

benz Veal
to ▇▇▇
10/8/2015 View details

Hey ▇▇▇,

in response to your email yesterday in regards to ▇▇▇▇▇ again. As i have said before, ▇▇▇ knows that i signed with ▇▇▇ 1st, across the board on a non exclusive contract for NYC, LA & Toronto before i signed with ▇▇▇ in LA as an LA based model and so technically, ▇▇▇ has jurisdiction over the New York market before ▇▇▇ but since they are non exclusive, they don't have a problem with you guys booking me work. When i decided to sign exclusively with ▇▇▇ for LA ONLY, for print and commercials, I informed ▇▇▇ of the matter and they were fine with it. For New York, ▇▇▇ never really got me much of anything on the print side because they knew i was doing more print work with ▇▇▇, the reason i said they're mostly TV. I just try to avoid going on auditions for them to prevent conflicts between you two because i am fully aware of the on going history of conflicts that you guys have with sharing models. but as i stated before, from time to time they book me stuff and in this case it happened to be ▇▇▇▇▇▇▇▇▇▇ was a direct booking through ▇▇▇. So therefore, i don't feel that i owe bella any commission on this particular job due to the non exclusivity for the New York market, but if i do owe the 20% commission fee, can you please explain to me how? Or produce a document that i signed stating that i was exclusive for print in the New York market with ▇▇▇, and if so, i have no problem paying the 300$ because i only want to do what's right. Thank you for your time, hope to hear back from you soon regarding this issue :-).

All the best,

R
▇▇▇▇▇▇
to me, ▇▇▇▇▇
10/13/2015 View details

Hi Benz-

Hope you had a nice weekend- I'm aware of your LA status with ▇▇▇ and ▇▇▇ LA. I guess I just thought that when you came to N.Y. these past few years that we would keep the exclusivity the same and quite frankly never thought of you signing any paper work so therefore you are right and not exclusive with us in New York. Moving forward, we will move you to our freelance board since you clarified your representation here in NY with ▇▇▇ having jurisdiction. We are fine with that.

Thanks

THE MACTOR'S GUIDE

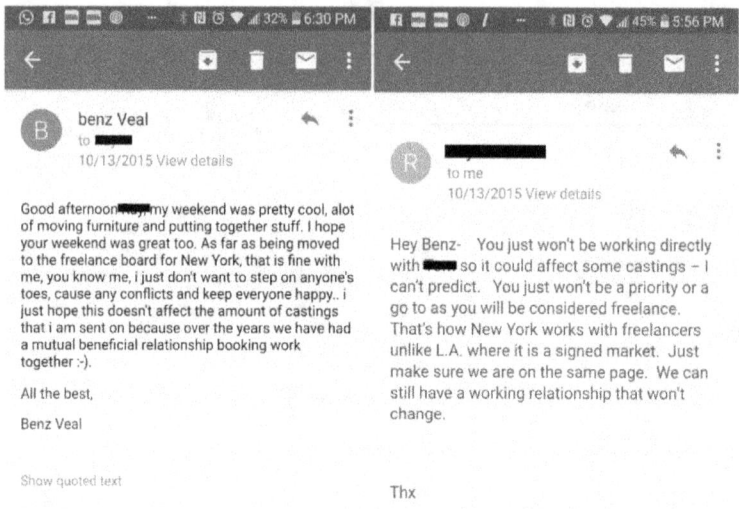

If I would've paid the $300 agency fee that I didn't owe, I'd probably still be working with that agent and making more money today. I reached out to the agent in the past, and he said that he didn't have a problem working with me, but it was up to the owner. The owner responded back saying that they were all set on the men's board but offered me the lifestyle board. I went in to visit them and talked with the agent that I had a strong relationship with. He expressed that he wishes that I was with them at the agency.

Don't make the same mistake that I made. You have to see the bigger picture and know that winning some battles today can result in you losing the war tomorrow. Luckily for me, it didn't ruin my career because I fortified myself with other agencies in different markets. I also had another agency in New York, but you may not be as lucky.

NO TO SERIOUS DATING
YES TO CASUAL DATING

People always ask me about dating. In my opinion, a Mactor shouldn't engage in a serious relationship at the **BEGINNING** of their career. My dad always told me that if you're going to do something, you should give it a 105%. It's hard to do that when you have someone else competing for your attention. It doesn't matter if someone is good or toxic for you; both of them cause a distraction.

When you're in a serious relationship; instead of working on a script, you're texting and talking to **THEM**. Instead of being in acting classes, you're going out to dinner with **THEM**. Instead of updating your profiles on casting sites, you're planning vacations with **THEM**. Instead of being at networking events, you're buying a pet for **THEM**. Instead of investing in new headshots, you're buying gifts for **THEM**. Instead of going to the gym, you're lying in bed with **THEM**, being lazy, getting fat and the list goes on. We've all heard the old saying *"one can't serve two masters."*

Casual dating is ok because it serves a purpose to clear up the monotony. This career can be stressful at times, so a little distraction isn't harmful.

Monotony: n. *A lack of change that makes something boring. (Webster's dictionary)*

With casual dating, you'll encounter life experiences that you can utilize in your career. I've met Mactors that were in successful relationships, but they weren't full-time models and actors and held a primary job.

Long distance serious relationships: Long distance relationships can be complicated. The fact that your partner will not be able to see you frequently will cause a strain on the relationship. People can become lonely and insecure. If you're attractive, that can create trust issues while you're away. I have tried long distance serious relationships before. They all started off well but ultimately failed because of the reasons aforementioned.

I was dating a woman for a while, and things were going great. She believed in me, my career and invested in my dream. That was the first time that I had ever met a woman that was willing to invest in me. I thought I had finally met someone that understood my crazy lifestyle as a traveling Mactor. After working 3 months in Africa, I returned back to the U.S and was ready to take the relationship to the next level. However, she felt another way and ultimately grew distant with me. Years later, she revealed that she was being young minded, insecure and felt like she wasn't the only one.

To date another Model/Actor: Some will say that dating another Mactor is better because they understand your lifestyle. They believe it would work versus dating people with regular jobs. There are some benefits to dating another Mactor. They understand your career; can help you memorize your lines, etc. However, like a casting director told me when I auditioned for a TV show in LA;

"Never date a model, actor or musician because they are selfish people."

    This is true, and I should've listened to the lady. One time I dated another Mactor seriously. At the time, she wasn't a full-time Mactor like me. She wasn't doing too much in her career. I really liked her personality and our chemistry, so I helped nurture her career. I gave her advice and showed her my ways. I brought her in on projects, and we would book jobs together because of our chemistry on set. Career-wise, it was a great relationship.

    I felt like I had found a protégé and we could grow together as a couple. However, on the personal side of our relationship, it was very toxic. I dealt with a lot of her insecurities from her previous failed relationships, envious behavior because of the success I had in my career, and she even viewed me as her competition.

    I was made to feel inadequate at times, and I stopped going to the gym like I usually would. The drive just wasn't there anymore. My financial debt had increased due to nurturing a failing relationship. The long distance didn't help because I was bi-coastal and she was only on the east coast. My dad told me to leave her alone because he noticed that I was stressed and lost my focus on my career, but I chose to stay with her.

    The relationship became worse between us. I finally ended the relationship. One day while she was on set, she told someone in production that our relationship had ended. It almost jeopardized a continuous job with that company for both of us. The company didn't know that we were a couple before that day. I found out because I had worked with the company alone one day and was asked about it by one of the production staff members.

I know that having a serious relationship while you are pursuing this career sounds excellent. However, it's time-consuming and takes a lot of work. Imagine what I could've accomplished if I would've spent that energy, time and money on my career, versus trying to have a serious relationship? Don't make this mistake. Keep your relationships casual until you've gained enough stability in your career or you're satisfied with what you've accomplished. Those men and women will still be there when you obtain your pot of gold at the end of the rainbow.

ALWAYS TRY TO PAY WHERE YOU LAY EVEN IF IT'S OFFERED FOR FREE

You never want to make people who offer you their place to stay, feel taken advantage of. When a friend offers you their place to stay for an extended amount of time, find a way to pay them. You can pay money, do handyman work around the house, buy them gifts, etc. Implement this strategy and you'll never wear out your welcome and can return if you need them again.

I always try to pay when a friend allows me to stay at their place for an extended period of time. If they don't accept my cash, I offer handyman work or surprise them with gifts to show my appreciation. Finding an affordable place to stay when you're relocating to different states for work can be difficult.

DON'T TAKE IT PERSONAL
IT'S JUST BUSINESS

You're a product to be sold to a consumer, and that consumer is a big company that wants to use your likeness to advertise their product to the masses. You're not going to book every job, so don't stress about it. You have to learn to move on and prepare for the next project. Early on in my career, I was sensitive about every audition. It stressed me out because I depended on it to pay my bills.

Once I developed the *attitude of not really caring anymore,* I started to book more jobs. Casting can see it in your eyes when you're desperate. What isn't right for you today will be right for you tomorrow. Don't take it personally. You will last a long time in the industry with this way of thinking.

BE ABOUT YOUR BUSINESS
AND YOUR BUSINESS WILL BE
ABOUT YOU

My dad always told me this, and it holds true. This will definitely work if you're giving a 105% percent to your craft. Opportunities will start gravitating towards you. When I am on top of my artistry, I find that opportunities just start rolling in. Your confidence is up, and you feel like you can conquer every audition and **YOU WILL!!**

DON'T GET YOUR HOPES UP

In this industry, people will promise you everything. They will tell you that they have a lot of connections and can connect you with people. Many people like to hear themselves talk. They like to offer what they can't provide. Don't fall for the hype. Hear what they're saying but don't accept it internally. Let them show you what they can do. I've met countless people that said they want to work with me, let's do lunch and talk about things but it never happened. Just keep moving forward in what you're trying to pursue, and the right people will come into your career path.

DON'T BE AFRAID TO CHANGE YOUR LOOK

One time in my career, it was hard for me to book young dad roles. I looked too young because my hair was cut low and didn't have any facial hair. I decided to start growing my head hair and facial hair. My agency didn't know what I was doing. One day I received an audition for Huggies. I went to the audition and booked the job. I showed up to the agency afterward with my hair grown out. I told my agent that I needed to grow my hair to look more like a young dad.

NETWORK! NETWORK! NETWORK!

This is an industry about who knows you. If you have excellent networking skills, you'll excel quickly. I still haven't mastered this skill because I'm part of the generation that believes that hard work alone, will take me to where I want to go.

I was raised to work and get whatever I want on my own and not ask for any help. In reality, talent can only take you so far. Your networking skills will carry you to the next level. Remember many terrible actors are working and some great actors who end up only as teachers. Don't be afraid to open your mouth and ask for help or anything you want. As the old saying goes; *"a closed mouth won't get fed."*

"Your appearance will get you the play, and your mind will get you paid."

UTILIZE SOCIAL MEDIA

This is another area I haven't mastered. I'm part of the old generation that solely depends on going to auditions to obtain work, so I don't have the energy to take selfies every day, buy new outfits and post pictures in them, make interesting and funny sketches or do silly performances for likes but **YOU DO!!** All of these things can bring in income and fame.

We are in the digital age so Instagram, YouTube; Facebook can catapult your career. When I'm at auditions, they immediately want to know your social media usernames. They want to see if you're an "*Influencer.*" They're looking at how many units they can sell if you market to your followers directly. Many people have secured great income by becoming social media famous. It has sprung forth actors as well. Models have been discovered and given lucrative paying contracts. Take advantage of this avenue.

Influencer: *n. a person with the ability to influence potential buyers of a product or services by promoting or recommending the items on social media. (Oxford Dictionary)*

- Develop a personal and a business Instagram page
- Develop a fan page on Facebook
- Develop a YouTube channel
- Develop a Twitter page

PHOTO LIBRARY

A photo library is when companies shoot concepts and sell your photos to anyone who wants to purchase them. This can help you or hurt you. It can help you if your career is slow because your photos will pop up anywhere, anytime and keep you relevant. It can hurt you because big companies can purchase your photos and use them and not have to pay you. Photo library companies only pay you once. Shooting photo libraries are similar to signing a perpetuity contract. You will grow old and still see your photos from that photo shoot. Shoot photo libraries only if you ***really need*** the money.

DON'T BE AFRAID OF TAXES

Many Mactors are petrified of taxes. I know because I used to be one of them. You don't have to fear taxes. Taxes are a Mactors best friend. The beautiful thing about taxes is; you can write off nearly everything. Most of your jobs are 1099 and not w-2. You're an independent contractor, so everything is an expense. Almost every breakfast, Lunch and dinner is a business meeting. Nearly every trip is a business trip. You can write off your agency commission fees, casting site charges, flight, bus and train tickets, clothes, personal website, and acting classes as expense write-offs. Your whole life is a write off as a full-time Mactor.

The expense that has the most impact on your federal taxes is your **vehicle mileage.** (if you own your vehicle)

"The more mileage you put on your car, the more it can take you from owing money to not owing money."

Pay for the Turbo Tax software. It will guide you through the process, step by step. I used to think it was hard, but it's quite simple and painless. Don't worry about keeping every receipt. Use your credit and debit card, so you can always pull up the receipts from your billing statements. Try to use one card for your career (preferably a credit card with cash back benefits).

CONCLUSION

This concludes this chapter and the end of this book. With the information that was given in this guide, you should have more than enough tools that you can utilize to aid you in this industry. Take what works for you and discard the rest. I am not a perfect person, and I'm not always right. What has worked for me, may not work for you. I went through a lot of trials and errors to figure out what works for me and I hope that this guide has brought you insight and a better understanding of the industry. It is a robust industry, but once you develop a strategy that works for you, it makes it a little easier. Everyone has their own path and experiences in this career. I am just happy that I can share mine and possibly help one of you gain success in yours. Thank you for taking the time to read this book and may your journey be filled with great success!!

MY SOCIAL MEDIA

EMAIL: themactorsguide@gmail.com

INSTAGRAM: @benzveal

TWITTER: @IamBENZVEAL

CLASSES

Here is a list of some classes that I've taken along my journey that you should check out.

HEY I SAW YOUR COMMERCIAL (On camera training)
5511 West Pico Blvd. Los Angeles, CA 90019
323.939.4612 www.heyisawyourcommercial.com
yourcommercialcoach@yahoo.com – Mike Pointer

BEVERLY HILLS PLAYHOUSE
254 S Robertson Blvd. Beverly Hills, CA 90211
310.855.1556 www.bhplayhouse.com

THE ACTORS CIRCLE
4475 Sepulveda Blvd. Culver City, CA 90230
310.837.4536 www.theactorscircle.com
Marcie Smolin

UPRIGHT CITIZENS BRIGADE SUNSET
5419 Sunset Blvd. Los Angeles, CA 90027
323.908.8702 www.sunset.ucbtheatre.com

GRAHAM SHIELS STUDIOS (On camera training)
5028 Wilshire Blvd. Suite #209 Los Angeles, CA 90036
323.252.6808 www.grahamshielsstudio.com

WEBSITES

ACTORS ACCESS: www.actorsaccess.com

LA CASTING: https://corp.castingnetworks.com/la/

CASTING FRONTIER: https://castingfrontier.com/

CAST IT TALENT: https://www.castittalent.com/

PHOTOGRAPHERS

Here is a list of some photographers that I have worked with along my journey that you should check out.

DANIEL D'OTTAVIO PHOTOGRAPHY
304 Boerum Street #25 Brooklyn, NY 11206
347.528.2263 www.danieldottavio.com
d@danieldottavio.com

DAN VILLAMAR STUDIO
www.dannyvillamarstudio.com
Seattle | Los Angeles | New York
Email for location: info@danvillamar.com

LALO TORRES NEW YORK
www.lalotorres.com
469.222.5030 lalo@lalotorres.com

NOEL DAGANTA PHOTOGRAPHY
1013 S Los Angeles St. Suite 1407 Los Angeles, CA 90015
818.793.4472 www.ndpictures.com
info@ndpictures.com

ROBERT OLIN STUDIOS
711 South Olive Street Suite 515 Los Angeles, CA 90014
323.437.5918 www.robertolin.com

RYLE WATSON (NYC, LA - Email for location)
www.rylewatson.com - R.Wastsonsp@gmail.com

PRIVATE COACHING

MARCUS FOLMAR (LA, NYC): booking.rm@gmail.com

AUDITION WITH SHAY MACK (self taping service)
1770 Richmond Circle Atlanta, GA 30315
678.216.7586 auditionwithshaymack@gmail.com

NOTES

www.ingramcontent.com/pod-product-compliance
Lightning Source LLC
Chambersburg PA
CBHW052213090526
44584CB00017BB/2299